The ESOP Company Board Handbook

The ESOP Company Board Handbook

Stephen P. Magowan
Scott Rodrick
Corey Rosen
John D. Schlichte
Cecil Ursprung
Michael Wade

The National Center for Employee Ownership
Oakland, California

The ESOP Company Board Handbook

Book design by Scott Rodrick

The National Center for Employee Ownership
1736 Franklin St., 8th Floor
Oakland, CA 94612
(510) 208-1300
Fax (510) 272-9510
www.nceo.org

First printed July 2009

ISBN-10: 1-932924-60-4
ISBN-13: 978-1-932924-60-2

Contents

Preface

Corey Rosen

In recent years, a growing number of ESOP companies have chosen to pay more attention to the structure and operations of their boards of directors. Part of this has been driven by changes in law and practice in boards of public companies, particularly in the wake of the Sarbanes-Oxley Act, passed in 2002. Although that law applies only to public companies, it has set a template private companies can use for what it means to have a professional and credible board.

The major driver, however, has been a growing recognition that boards can be very important in helping assure the long-term success of a company. In the past, ESOPs were often transitional vehicles used to buy out an owner, only to be terminated some years later when the company was sold to deal with the ESOP repurchase obligation or take advantage of an attractive offer. Today, more and more companies want to stay ESOP-owned for the long term, a change driven in large part by the advent of 100% S corporation ESOPs.

Effective boards, especially those with outside members, can provide a number of benefits, including:

- Bring fresh perspectives, business contacts, and credibility to the governance process.
- Help to manage executive compensation in an effective and balanced way.
- Help assure that any proposed acquisitions by or of an ESOP company are consistent with the best interests of shareholders.
- Provide a place to seek a more objective resolution of internal corporate conflicts.
- Help management focus on such crucial issues as repurchase obligation and corporate culture.

- Make sure the ESOP fiduciary is doing the job well and, particularly, acting for the interests of participants rather than other interests.

Having served on one corporate board and now serving on another, I have seen these issues first hand. Serving on any corporate board is a serious responsibility. Serving on an ESOP company board adds the additional responsibility of understanding how ESOP law and best practices interact with corporate law and best practices. Special ESOP issues such as valuation, the repurchase obligation, S corporation anti-abuse rules, monitoring fiduciaries, stricter considerations for executive pay, changes in corporate capitalization, and responding to takeover bids, among others, demand at least a working knowledge of ESOP requirements.

This book is designed to help board members navigate through these issues. You will learn basic ESOP rules as well as how ESOP boards actually function from interviews with a number of outside directors, what your corporate and ESOP responsibilities are, how to think about executive pay, and a number of other issues. In addition to this book, the NCEO offers recorded Webinars on effective boards and ESOP basics. You can also contact us to meet with you to discuss these issues further.

Despite the added responsibility of serving on an ESOP company board, there are great rewards as well. ESOP companies are often leaders in their fields, with a genuine commitment to create a new kind of workplace that places special value on the contributions of all employees. It is a great privilege to serve on a board of a company like this and be involved in this exciting endeavor.

CHAPTER 1

Governing the ESOP Company: Fiduciary Issues and Practical Solutions for Boards of Directors in ESOP Companies

Stephen P. Magowan

Members of the ESOP community generally believe that our companies are different from other companies. Many studies indicate that our sense of difference is indeed a valid one as ESOP companies that have high employee involvement in work-level decisions and open-book management last longer, perform better, and provide better benefits than similarly situated non-ESOP companies.[1] These facts are well-known to ESOP enthusiasts—not only the many legal, accounting, and business consultants in the ESOP field, but also the employees of the many successful ESOP companies that have embraced the culture of sharing financial information and incorporating the needs of employees and the surrounding community into the consideration of the daily life of the basic capitalistic enterprise of selling things or services for more than what it costs to produce.

This is no mere stuff. A close examination of the emerging ESOP community, now well into its fourth decade, reveals a hint of a new capitalism—a common or shared capitalism, one might call it, that can be embraced by liberals and conservatives alike because an ownership culture deeply rooted in community is still, nevertheless, a culture based in capitalism. Fostered by the generous tax benefits offered by the ESOP

1. See, e.g., Joseph Blasi and Douglas Kruse, "Economic Performance and Employee Ownership, Profit Sharing, and Stock Options: The NBER Study," *Journal of Employee Ownership Law and Finance* vol. 20, no. 3 (fall 2008): 31–40; Corey M. Rosen, "Equity: Why Employee Ownership Is Good for Business," in Robert W. Smiley, Jr. et al., eds., *Employee Stock Ownership Plans* (Washington, D.C.: Beyster Institute, 2007), vol. 1.

structure in the 1970s, i.e., capital gains tax deferrals, the income tax deductibility of dividends, and the conversion of principal payments on loans to an income tax deduction, and now accelerated by the advent of the tax-free ESOP-owned S corporation structure,[2] this new capitalism now seems to have placed us in the midst of a revolution.[3]

Notwithstanding these suppositions, the legal standards governing the conduct of members of boards of directors of ESOP-owned companies hark back to a legal history that has little or nothing to do with ESOPs, employee ownership, or a new-styled capitalism. These standards, governing a board's duty of care, duty of loyalty, the business judgment rule, and the basic legal framework underlying the governance of corporations in general, have historical roots dating to the Gilded Age of the late 19th century, though they have been revised over time through statutory changes and judicial interpretation.

An understanding of these rules is essential for the good governance of an ESOP-owned company,[4] regardless of whether the ESOP is a minority or majority holder. This understanding will enable board members to approach their role on an informed basis rather than in a vacuum.

In addition to understanding these rules, a member of a corporation's board of directors must also be aware of the federal ERISA[5] fiduciary issues that cover ESOPs and how these rules intersect and sometimes lead to conflicting modes of operation.

---

2. This is an advantage that some very skilled observers of tax policy believe to be an abomination. See Martin D. Ginsburg and Jack S. Levin, *Mergers, Acquisitions and Buyouts*, July 2008 ed. (Wolters Kluwer, 2008), vol. 2, ¶ 1102.2.1, at pp. 11–17 ("We continue to believe the one really sensible legislative change . . . would repeal the 1996 legislation classifying ESOPs . . . as eligible [S corporation] shareholders.").

3. For additional thoughts on this emerging revolution, see Gar Alperovitz, *America: Beyond Capitalism* (Hoboken, NJ: John Wiley & Sons, 2005), 81–89.

4. In this chapter, a reference to "ESOP-owned" includes both a minority ESOP-owned company and a majority ESOP-owned company unless the text otherwise makes a distinction.

5. All references to ERISA are to the Employee Retirement Income Security Act of 1974 as amended through November 30, 2008, and to the regulations thereunder.

In reviewing all of these rules, a board member would do well to bear in mind how case law gets made. Judicial decisions on fiduciary matters are made by the application of legal principles to the facts presented in the court. The presentation of facts to the court, however, very seldom reflects how facts were received by board members. Frequently, the only persons ever to receive a clearly articulated and sequentially summarized statement of fact are the judge and jury after the fact.

When board members are in the midst of a rushed corporate transaction or a consideration of how to rescue a financially challenged business, they will not, as a rule, enjoy the luxury of learning the facts and subtle issues of their situation over a period of days and weeks. Board members, by and large, receive facts in bursts and often under conditions of extreme pressure. It will not be surprising, then, that what a board needs more than almost anything else is a clearly articulated set of standards and processes to guide not only its everyday work but also how it will handle such things as a fully funded offer to purchase the company, an economic downturn in the business, or a loss of confidence in a key executive.

The Goal of This Chapter

The goal of this chapter is to create for board members a foundation of principles and processes that can guide them as directors in the day-to-day operations of being a member of the board of directors of a corporation with an ESOP shareholder as well as in special situations such as those articulated above. This chapter also offers some forward-looking suggestions about how ESOP-owned companies *should* be governed as opposed to how they *can* be governed.

We in the ESOP community can learn a lot from studying the general principles of corporate governance espoused in statutory and case law relating to public and private non-ESOP companies. I will use a review of these principles to ask why we use the principles we use, what the sources of those principles are, and whether ESOP companies could develop models beyond those principles to obtain better results.

Thus, this chapter will proceed with a general examination of the definition of a board of directors, a review of the general obligations of the board, and a consideration of the duty of care and duty of loyalty. It will consider the obligation of good faith and the emergence of Sarbanes-Oxley. These rules will set the baseline for the discussion that follows as I focus on the reality of how boards work inside the boardroom and how information flows to and from the board.

I will examine how courts and legislatures have reviewed directors' decisions in non-ESOP settings such as the sale of a business and the approach of insolvency. The focus will include a review of the closely held private corporation and how, starting in the late 1950s and early 1960s, the courts and legislatures began to realize that boards of directors of closely held corporations should be held to different (frequently higher) standards than boards of publicly traded corporations. I consider whether this change in the law is a model for questioning whether ESOP companies need their own set of rules.

This chapter also turns at various times to the ESOP company itself. I will examine how boards of directors should view their roles in light of the governing case law and in light of what an ESOP company ought to be striving for. I will focus on such areas as:

- How should a board review the considerations for an initial ESOP transaction? A second-stage transaction? A final-stage transaction?
- How should a board review particular considerations in ESOP transactions such as the issuance of warrants, stock appreciation rights, and the like?
- How should a board oversee the compensation of the CEO? Should it also review compensation for other senior officers?
- What kind of training should board members have on specific ESOP issues?
- What are the best practices in the composition and selection of the board?
- How can a board use committees to govern an ESOP-owned company more effectively?
- At what level should a board be involved in reviewing leases, employment agreements, consulting arrangements, and the like?
- Should a board have separate legal representation from the company's counsel for transactions? What about generally?

- How should a board handle a potential sale of an ESOP-owned company?
- What about the multiple-hat question? We know that some individuals serve as an officer, a director, and an ESOP trustee, but how can they do so effectively? What legal standard governs their conduct?
- Is there a board role in maintaining ESOP culture?
- Who should select a board? How can a board handle its own succession planning?
- Is a board's role to support a CEO or to challenge him or her?
- What is a board's relationship to other senior management?
- What is a board's relationship to ESOP participants generally?

This chapter will include a bit of contemplation, asking, "If we could construct a reasonably perfect model of ESOP company governance, what would it look like?" While recognizing that it is not possible to construct a perfect ESOP corporation governance model that can be applied like some kind of paint-by-numbers kit writ large, this chapter will try to show that the effort of building the model can have sanguinary results. Surely, the effort to derive some general principles is a worthwhile endeavor that will enable us to continue the steady march forward of this unique brand of American capitalism.

The Emergence of the Corporate Form

Before the ESOP, there was the corporation. The corporate form as we know it with shareholders, directors, and officers is a creation of statutory law. This is a subtle but important point. Statutory law arises because the people, through their legislatures, decide to do something. It is not law made by judges. It is not an inherited understanding (in lawyers' lingo, the "common law").

Corporations arose in large part because a growing need for investment capital meant that there needed to be an entity that could protect investors so that when they created an enterprise, their entire financial lives (homes, savings, etc.) were not at risk if the company failed. As a separate legal entity, a corporation offered limitation of liability.

In return for creating this privilege, the states determined to make sure that shareholder rights were protected and that certain public interests were guarded as well (ultimately, this included making corporations taxable). In other words, the corporation did not just spring into existence, but rather arose out of the determined decisions of legislative bodies elected by the people.

Shareholder Voting Rights: The Foundational Principles

The various states approached the formation of corporate law in fundamentally different ways. For example, some states allowed corporations to exist only for a period of time or to perform only specific acts enumerated in the articles of incorporation. Further, some states placed strict limits on the limitation of liability offered by the corporation.[6] By and large, however, one consistently applied principle in the emerging body of corporate law was that corporations would function as mini versions of representative democracies.

What did this mean? Under state corporation law, shareholders are voters. But rather than voting on the principle of "one man, one vote," they vote on the principle of "one share, one vote." Hence, in a corporation the vote follows share ownership, and economic control translates into voting control. Whom do the shareholders elect? The shareholders elect the board of directors. The board of directors in turn oversees the operations of the corporation.

Here, I think it is useful to take a little bit of a historical diversion to review the substance of "shareholder voting rights." Although state legislatures in the United States created the form of representative democracy in the corporation, as corporations got bigger, they very rapidly became dissociated from the base of shareholders, and state legislatures offered virtually no additional protections to shareholders. Thus, it was not until the federal securities acts of the 1930s (which emerged from the evaporation of shareholder wealth from 1929 to 1933) that shareholder voting rights became anything more than symbolic.

---

6. California, for example, imposed pro-rata liability on shareholders of California corporations for unpaid debts until the 1930s. Franklin Gevurtz, *Corporation Law* (St. Paul, MN: West, 2000), 28.

Corporations also emerged very rapidly as centers of power and wealth. Economic wealth in the United States in the late 19th century rapidly consolidated in the hands of enterprising industrialists and financiers who formed various combines and trusts across industries. With this concentration came alternating cycles of boom and bust, monopolies, corruption, and often dreadful working conditions. By the early 20th century, big business faced a rising tide of dissent from government regulators, labor reformers, and others.[7] It was over the ensuing several decades that competing visions of how to harness economic growth—for example, totally "free" enterprise vs. an enterprise society based on nationalism vs. state-run "collective enterprise"—that the current pattern of corporate regulation emerged, including federal requirements for boards and other aspects of corporate governance. These rules, however, almost exclusively focused on publicly traded companies.

These regulatory compromises sought to balance the interests of shareholders with respect to redress for harm against what was perceived as the viable functioning of the corporation. And so, fundamentally, this is how the legal oversight over the relationship between shareholders and the boards they selected was birthed, at least at the federal level. Most of the rules for privately held corporations were still based on state statutory and case law.

The state law governing fiduciary relationships in privately held companies (or "close corporations") largely paralleled federal law. However, beginning in the late 1950s, a number of legal writers posited the idea that close corporations were different and that the fiduciary issues in such corporations should be handled differently. Perhaps the leading early voice in this movement was Professor F. Hodge O'Neal, first alone and then with co-author Professor Robert Thompson, whose major treatises *Close Corporations* and *Oppression of Minority Shareholders* articulated the now largely accepted position that directors in a close corporation owe a special duty to minority shareholders and that shareholders in a close corporation are more like partners owing each other mutual fiduciary duties than they are like shareholders who are distant from one another in a large publicly traded corporation. I will return to this concept later.

---

7. See, e.g., J. Anthony Lukas, *Big Trouble* (New York City: Touchstone, 1997).

Basic Operative Principles for a Board of Directors: Sources of Law and an Overview of the State Statutes

The basic governing legal principles for board members arise from four sources: (1) state statutory law governing corporations; (2) a corporation's articles of incorporation (or "articles of association" as they are called in some states); (3) the corporation's bylaws; and (4) the state's case law concerning board fiduciary matters such as the duty of care, the duty of loyalty, and the business judgment rule. The state law that will govern the internal operations of the corporation, including board matters, is the law of the state of incorporation of the corporation in question.

Many corporations simply file articles of incorporation in the state where the principal business of the corporation began. Some states, however, with Delaware generally the acknowledged leader, aggressively modified their statutes to make corporate formation and operation easier and, in many instances, to offer broader fiduciary protections to board members. In some circles, Delaware's changes were viewed as initiating a "race to the bottom" that eviscerated shareholder rights over time. Some corporations intentionally incorporate in Delaware or other states in order to take advantage of more flexible corporate laws.

State laws require a company to have a board of directors[8] and generally contain a provision similar to the following when describing the corporate powers exercised by the board:

---

8. 11A Vt. Stat. Ann. § 8.01(a). In this chapter I primarily cite the corporate statutory law of the state of Vermont, the state where I practice. Vermont's statute is based on the Model Business Corporation Act with some minor, immaterial changes. The provisions found in Vermont law will by and large be found in other state corporation laws. Many state corporation laws permit so-called "close corporations" to do away with the board of directors. See, e.g., 11A Vt. Stat. Ann. §§ 20.20.01, et seq. Such corporations are permitted to operate without a board of directors and permit the shareholders to agree to regulate the exercise of corporate powers through shareholder agreements. It is doubtful whether the election of closed corporations status would be a wise option for a company with an ESOP.

> All corporate powers shall be exercised by, or under the authority of, and the business and affairs of the corporation manage under the direction of, its board of directors, subject to any limitation set forth in the articles of incorporation.[9]

Statutory law also contains rules governing the minimum number of directors, the terms of directors, the impact of vacancy on boards, and how directors meet.

Three key principles that arise from most corporate law statutes are as follows:

1. *Actions without meeting*. Most state corporate laws permit a board of directors to act without actually meeting. This means that the boards can agree on something in writing that all board members sign, thereby creating an efficient way for boards of directors to conduct routine business. In general it is not mandatory to allow actions without meetings, and it can be prohibited within the articles of incorporation or bylaws.
2. *Creation of committees*. Most state statutes permit a board of directors to adopt committees. The committees can perform board functions and must have two or more board members on the committee. The use of committees is an important aspect in the evolving notions of corporate governance. However, most state statutes will prohibit committees from taking certain actions such as authorizing distributions and dividends, filling vacancies on the board, amending the articles of incorporation, or approving merger plans.[10]
3. *Articles can contain any legal rules*. State corporation laws include provisions that allow a corporation to adopt any provisions that are not inconsistent with law. This allows corporations to develop individualized standards and procedures of governance.

The board is elected by the shareholders at an annual meeting. It is possible that all directors will stand for election each year, though many corporations have bylaw provisions that allow for staggered

9. 11A Vt. Stat. Ann. § 8.01(b).

10. See 11A Vt. Stat. Ann. § 8.25.

elections so that only a portion of the board is elected in a given year in order to limit turnover.

Because the board is elected by the shareholders, it is logical to suppose that the board merely represents the interests of the shareholders and that the board will engage in the kind of constituent work that elected political representatives often engage in. But that is not the case. In large publicly traded corporations, officers of the company frequently control the election of the board, though the emergence of Sarbanes-Oxley and the corporate scandals since the late 1990s have led some boards to become more independent.

In close corporations, board members are also frequently shareholders and officers and view themselves more as partners to each other in the enterprise rather than as representing any shareholder's interest *per se* other than his or her own.[11] The introduction of the ESOP as a shareholder into a closely held corporation,[12] however, creates a constituent where none had previously existed. Of necessity, the introduction of a new constituent should result in changed relationships between the board and shareholders. This does not always happen, though, and that presents a problem. I will turn back to the nature of board relations to shareholders in the closely held corporate setting repeatedly throughout this chapter.

Many state corporate law statutes also include a statutory description of the general standards that will govern boards of directors. The statutes generally require that a director will discharge his or her duties as a director in good faith, with the care an ordinarily prudent person in a like position would exercise under similar circumstances and in a manner the director reasonably believes to be in the best interest of the corporation.[13] What is important here is that the director is being held to the standard of an "ordinarily prudent person." The director is not held to the standard of an expert.

---

11. See generally F. Hodge O'Neal and Robert B. Thompson, *O'Neal and Thompson's Oppression of Minority Shareholders and LLC Members*, rev. 2d ed. (St. Paul, MN: West, 2008).

12. In this chapter, I refer to "privately held" and "closely held" interchangeably. I use both phrases to define the ownership of a corporation whose shares are not publicly traded on any stock exchange.

13. See 11A Vt. Stat. Ann. § .30(a).

Because the director is only supposed to meet the prudent person test, the standard of conduct statutes also allow a director to rely on information, reports, and statements prepared or presented by one or more officers or employees of the corporation. To be able to rely on these reports, however, the director must reasonably believe that the person is reliable and competent in the matters presented. Directors may also rely on advice from legal counsel, public accountants, and other professionals. In addition, a board member is generally entitled to rely on a committee of the board of directors of which the director is not a member if the director reasonably believes that the committee is competent.

A director is not generally considered to be acting in good faith if he or she has actual knowledge concerning the matter in question that makes the reliance outlined immediately above unwarranted. For example, if a director were a CPA and could tell that reports presented to the board were not accurate from an accounting perspective, he or she would be held to a higher standard. Finally, a director is generally not liable for any action taken as a director or any failure to act if he or she performed these actions in conformance with the statutory section.[14]

General Review of Articles of Incorporation and Bylaws

As noted above, the board of directors is responsible for the oversight of the corporation's operations and in that role appoints the officers of the corporation who handle the day-to-day business operations. State corporate statutes, however, provide little guidance to boards as to how to conduct this oversight function. Instead it creates a kind of open architecture that the board and shareholders can best fill in. This "filling in" generally takes place in the context of the articles of incorporation and the corporation's bylaws.

The foundational documents of a corporation are its articles of incorporation and bylaws. Board members must become familiar with both documents. The typical articles of incorporation are brief, perhaps naming the corporation, the number and type of shares the

14. See 11A Vt. Stat. Ann. § 8.30(d); Del. Gen. Corp. Law § 141(e).

corporation can issue, the number of directors it may have, and the address of the corporation's registered agent.

State corporation laws also permit the articles of incorporation to include myriad other provisions, a number of which can be useful for ESOP-owned companies. For example, the corporation statute for a given state is likely to permit the articles to include provisions that are not otherwise contrary to law regarding:

- the purpose for which the corporation is organized;
- the scope of power of directors, officers and shareholders, including creating special voting groups, supermajority provisions, limiting the power of a board to amend the articles, and setting the compensation of the board;
- the creation of special classes of shares and the rights associated with such special classes; and
- the limiting of liability of a board member to the corporation or its shareholders for money damages except for (1) any amount of financial benefit received by the director to which he or she was not entitled; (2) liability associated with intentional or reckless infliction of harm on the corporation; (3) liability associated with a director's intentional or reckless criminal act or (4) liability associated with the directors voting to make distributions to shareholders in violation of the corporations act.[15]

The bylaws of a corporation contain the provisions for the management of the corporation. Bylaws may include any provisions that are not inconsistent with the law or with the articles of incorporation.[16] Typically, the bylaws of a corporation include the provisions for the appointment of directors, the number of directors, how directors meet (whether, for instance, meetings by telephone are permitted), and whether the board shall have committees and what the roles of those committees shall be. Bylaws also contain provisions about how shareholders will conduct the meeting of shareholders and whether

---

15. See generally 11A Vt. Stat. Ann. § 2.02.

16. See 11A Vt. Stat. Ann. § 2.06.

they can act by written consent. In addition, the bylaws will name and define the officers' positions, such as president, vice president, and so forth.

Much of what may be contained in the articles of incorporation may also be contained in the bylaws, and vice versa. For boards of directors, a key consideration in reviewing what to include in the articles of incorporation and bylaws is understanding how the two are amended. For the most part, articles of incorporation can be amended only by a vote of both the directors and the shareholders. Accordingly, if a provision is put in the articles of incorporation, it is more challenging to take out.[17] In general, however, bylaws can be amended by the board of directors without shareholder input, though some corporation statutes give the ability to amend to the shareholders as well as the directors.[18]

The General Duties of a Board of Directors

I now turn to an examination and review of the legal duties of a board of directors as outlined in statutory and case law. In general, these duties are the duty of care, the duty of loyalty, and the duty to act in good faith as outlined under state law. In addition, there is emerging law from the passage of Sarbanes-Oxley in 2002 that is affecting privately held companies.[19] In this context, I will review to whom the various duties are owed and whether there are times when the constituency for whom the board acts changes. Once these duties are reviewed, I will examine how boards of directors exercise these duties and look at the effect of and protection offered by the "business judgment rule."

---

17. Note, however, that a vote to amend the articles of incorporation is not generally a vote that must pass through to beneficiaries of the ESOP under Internal Revenue Code Section 409 unless, for example, the vote would also be deemed to create a recapitalization.

18. See 11A Vt. Stat. Ann. § 10.20(b).

19. Sarbanes-Oxley Act of 2002, H.R. 3763, 107th Cong., 2d Sess ("SOX"). Although SOX applies only to publicly traded companies, its principles are seen as having application to close corporations and nonprofit corporations. Board members would likely be wise to understand the basics of SOX, as its standards may ultimately end up being more far-reaching than planned by Congress.

The Duty of Care

The duty of care is easy to state but not so easy to define. A relatively simple statement of the duty of care is that directors of a corporation have to exercise their duties in a way that avoids harm to the corporation. The duty of care requires that board members be attentive to the operations of the company. Courts tend to describe the duty of care as the duty to act as a reasonably prudent person would act under similar circumstances. However, certain statutory rules and the concept of the "business judgment rule" create some limitations on the application of the prudent person rule.

Let us first look at some general principles. Under the duty of care, a board of directors has to maintain attentiveness to the operations of the corporation. In other words, a board member may not be an empty suit. He or she must keep a proverbial eye on the clock. A quick review of a case from 1981 demonstrates how *not* to do this.

In *Francis v. United Jersey Bank*, 87 N.J. 15, 432 A.2d 814 (1981), a Mrs. Pritchard was a board member of a corporation largely run by her two sons. Unfortunately, Mrs. Pritchard drank heavily and did nothing to inform herself of what was happening with the business while her sons were conveniently borrowing money from the corporation and driving it into debt that it could not pay. Eventually, the corporation went bankrupt, and Mrs. Pritchard was sued by creditors for not exercising her duty of care. The court found that Mrs. Pritchard had breached her duty and owed damages to the corporation (funds that the corporation in turn would pay to the creditors).

In making this decision, the court made some important observations. First, the court determined that a director must have at least a rudimentary understanding of the business of the corporation. Second, the court stated that directors have to keep informed of the operations of the corporation. They must attend board meetings and, further, they must inform themselves as to what is going on in those board meetings. Finally, according to the court, directors must review on a regular basis the financial statements of the corporation.

So, although the facts of the *Francis* case are rather unique and extreme, the court articulates three basic rules that are universal:

1. "Know thy company." A board member must understand the company's general business, its business cycle, and its competition. A board member should be capable of determining who the significant competition is, what makes the year a successful year or a failure, and what external and internal forces could affect the business positively or negatively. If the business is in a technical field, the board member needs to develop an understanding of that technical field. If the board member finds that he or she cannot grasp the field, then the course is simple—that board member should step down from the board.
2. "Know thy company's operations." In addition to having a 30,000-foot-level understanding of the company and its prospects, the board member must be able to understand what is happening currently, on a quarter-by-quarter and annual basis. For example, the board member should know who the key employees are, what they do, what their strengths and limitations are, how they are performing, how they are compensated, and whether they are subject to non-compete and non-solicitation agreements.
3. "Know thy company's financials." A board member needs to know how the company stands vis-à-vis its earnings and its creditors, including its principal bank and trade creditors. It is not enough to know the company's sales; a board member needs to know the company's profit picture and whether it is meeting its obligations, including its relevant financial covenants.

The court in *Francis* also acknowledged that different circumstances may lead to different decisions. Thus, in looking at the duty of care, one must also consider the type of business the corporation is involved in, as the duty of care for one type of corporation may be different from another type. For example, courts reviewing the duty of care for directors of banking corporations have typically held them to a higher standard of care.[20] Further, board members who are also executives may be held to a higher standard because of the expectation that they will have more knowledge. Finally, in one case that has been subject to some criticism, a Delaware court ruled that if a corporation

20. See *Medford Trust Co. v. McKnight*, 292 Mass. 1 197 N.E. 649 (Mass. 1935).

were extremely large, then the board's role would be limited to broad policy decisions rather than supervision of day-to-day activities, and, accordingly, its duty of care would be more circumscribed than that of a board of a smaller corporation.[21]

Statutory Rules Relating to the Duty of Care

Most state corporate statutes include provisions that relate to the duty of care, and many statutes provide explicitly that the duty of care is based on a prudent person standard. Also, as noted, under the Model Business Corporation Act, there is a provision allowing directors to rely in good faith on records and reports of subordinates as well as opinions of outside advisors.[22] This is intended to provide some sort of statutory defense for directors. In addition, other states have either raised the bar for liability from general standards of negligence or put damage caps on suits against directors.[23] Companies can also put into their articles of incorporation provisions that limit liability for breach of fiduciary duties of boards of directors to actions that constitute gross negligence, recklessness, and the like.[24]

---

21. *Graham v. Dallis-Chalmers Mfg. Co.*, 41 Del. Ch. 78, 188 A.2d 125 (1963).
22. *Model Business Corporation Act* § 8.30(b).
23. See generally Ind. Cod. Ann. § 23-1-35(1)(e)(2) (raising the bar for liability); Va. Code Ann. § 13.1-692.1(A)(2) (putting a cap of $100,000 on the director's compensation).
24. Most corporations do this as a matter of "boilerplate" adoption of the articles of incorporation prepared by company counsel. There is, however, an interesting query here for ESOP trustees. If a corporation limits its board of directors' duty of care in such a manner, should the value of the company be discounted? Should an ESOP trustee require that articles containing these provisions be amended to take out the limitation of liability? Arguably, if directors' liability is limited in this fashion, they would be less attentive. If they are less attentive, then they are not being as careful as they need to be to make certain that the corporation's performance is at a level that would support the valuation. It seems logical, but I question whether any trustee ever pursues this argument.

To Whom Is the Duty Owed?

A director generally owes his or her duty of care to the corporation, but this constituency expands to the shareholders in the context of mergers and to creditors if the corporation is facing significant financial difficulties. Thus, if a corporation is near insolvency, the director's duties may run to the creditors of the corporation, because otherwise the shareholders may take such risks with the corporation that the creditor constituency may be harmed.[25] When a company engages in a leveraged buyout, determining to whom the duties lie is complicated. For example, in a case involving RJR Nabisco, the court held that the board had no duty to pre-existing bond holders in the leveraged buyout even though the buyout affected them greatly.[26]

Some states have passed so-called "other constituency" statutes. These statutes generally only apply to publicly held companies and allow boards of directors to consider the impact of their decisions on constituencies such as employees and local economies. While these rules generally only apply to publicly traded corporations, most state corporation statutes are drafted so that a corporation may include in its articles of incorporation any legal provision. Arguably, even a privately held company, such as one held only by an ESOP or only by individual shareholders and an ESOP, could include such provisions in its articles or certificate of incorporation.

Summary

In summary, the duty of care requires directors to inform themselves and to act reasonably. This is a common-sense concept. A director is a fiduciary for other people and sits in a role to protect the interest of the people who elected him or her, i.e., the shareholders. To exercise his or her duty of care, a director should ask some very basic questions and get some very basic understandings:

---

25. See generally *Credit Lyonnais Bank Nederland, N.V. v. Pathé Communications Corp.*, 191 WL 277613 (Del. Ch. 1991).

26. See generally *Metropolitan Life Ins. Co. v. RJR Nabisco, Inc.*, 716 F. Supp. 1504 (S.D.N.Y. 1989).

1. Directors should understand the business financials. Initially that may require a new director to receive more than just perfunctory reports, such as training in understanding the business financials.
2. The director should understand how the business works. Beyond the dollars, the director should know what it is that makes the business earn money. What market conditions help the business, and what market conditions hurt the business? What typically determines whether the business has a good selling season or not? What are the cycles to the business? What are the personality traits in key executive positions in the company that help it succeed? What are the personality traits that prevent it from succeeding?
3. The director should also actively be involved in the strategic planning of the business. The director's role is clearly to set broad policy in the context of the strengths and weaknesses of the business and the threats and opportunities that face it.

Does the Duty of Care Change When an ESOP Becomes a Shareholder? Should It Change? What Can/Should a Board of Directors with an ESOP Do Differently?

As noted above, the concept of the duty of care is not immutable; that is to say, it is not a principle that applies uniformly to all factual situations. Thus a board member of a bank has a different kind of duty of care than a board member of a firm that makes office furniture. A board member's duty of care is also different whenever there is an ESOP shareholder.

I come to this conclusion in several ways. First, general negligence theory is founded on the concept that if a fiduciary breaches a duty to a person to whom the fiduciary owed a duty (let's say a duty of care), then the fiduciary is liable for the harm caused by his or her breach. Also, under general negligence rules, if a fiduciary knows that this person has a particular trait that makes it possible that he or she can be harmed more easily or in a different way, then the fiduciary's duty is enhanced to take into account the special trait.

Second, in any corporation, common sense tells us that the board of directors must be responsive to the needs of significant shareholders.

If an ESOP owns, say, a 25% or larger equity stake and has provided the method through which the corporation's founder has had a liquidity event, then it seems logical that the board should be paying special attention to that ESOP's needs.

There are two useful corollaries that come to mind here. First, when a private equity firm provides a liquidity event for an owner, the private equity firm frequently obtains significant if not majority control over the board, and the business is largely run to meet the investment return expectations of the private equity investor, e.g., the need for a second liquidity event in X years.

The second corollary relates to the doctrine of "reasonable expectations." Under this doctrine, a minority shareholder's reasonable expectations that formed when it invested in the corporation are to be protected from improper or abusive exercises of majority control. Thus, although a majority shareholder may by virtue of his or her majority position have the power to do what he or she wants with the corporation, his or her actions are limited by a fiduciary relationship to the minority shareholder, and the scope of that relationship is measured by the reasonable expectations of the minority shareholder. Thus, the director's (and majority shareholders') duty to the ESOP would specifically relate to the ESOP's expectation when it invested in the company, for example, in connection with a leveraged ESOP transaction.

Here is where things get interesting. In the many cases where individual plaintiffs have alleged frustration of reasonable expectations, it is virtually impossible to have any true objective basis for determining these expectations. This is not true in the ESOP setting because in the ESOP setting we have the valuation report prepared for the ESOP trustee, which is nearly always based in significant part on the projections of future financial growth of the business. So, if the ESOP trustee is basing its purchase on those forecasted financials, it is reasonable to say that the ESOP—as a shareholder—at least has a reasonable expectation that the company will take steps to meet those forecasts. So, if the board takes actions that lower the projected earnings, for example by making bonuses to executives, the board will be violating a duty of care owed to the ESOP shareholder.

Here, however, we run into a problem arising from the received wisdom of how ESOP purchase transactions are conducted. As a general rule, a professional (i.e., bank) trustee does not share any analyses performed for it by its appraiser in the ESOP purchase transaction. Realizing this is not without controversy, is it completely against the interests of the ESOP participants for the directors to understand how the ESOP trustee arrived at a "yes" answer to the transaction after the fact within the context of making certain the directors and the ESOP are on the same page concerning the ESOP's expectations? If a person is a director of a corporation that has an ESOP as a shareholder, I think it is necessarily obvious that the director needs to understand how that shareholder is different and needs to understand what that shareholder's expectations were when it became a shareholder.

Here are a few specific suggestions for how the board should undertake this next level of examination and understanding:

1. *The board needs to understand the ESOP.* The board needs to understand the tax ramifications and business and general financial implications of having an ESOP, particularly the repurchase obligation. Reports about the ESOP should be as critical to board decision-making as reports about the business, and the board should consider policies that will provide for measured growth of the share value of the company and that take into account any retirement bulges that might exist within the employee populace.
2. *The board needs to learn how the ESOP became a shareholder.* What were the terms of the transaction? What were the forecasts that supported the valuation? How was the business described to the trustee/buyer? Has that business changed? Have the forecasts been met?
3. *The board needs to learn about the intersection between their duties as directors and the ESOP trustee's duties under ERISA.* The board should learn where its duties generally begin and end (i.e., on general corporation matters) and where the ESOP trustees' duties begin and end (on all matters involving the ESOP). If board members are also trustees, then they should assume that they will be held to a high duty of responsibility to the ESOP.
4. *The board needs to understand how choices made by executives of the company can affect the value of the shares held by the ESOP and actively take part in helping to structure those decisions.* Here is an egregious

example. If an executive knows that he or she is retiring soon and that the company has a lump-sum cash-out provision under its ESOP, then that executive may take risks to pump up the share value. If the board does not appreciate the existence of the lump-sum payment provision, it might not realize that it should hold back some of what the executive wants to do. Further, if the executive has compensation in the form of stock appreciation rights, that executive's desire for an increased value in the stock appreciation rights may be at odds with a more reasonable growth pattern.

5. *The board must develop a balanced approach between protecting assets and committing capital to the company's growth.* By and large, the ESOP should help the board adopt a middle approach that blends a desire to commit capital to expand business with a need to preserve capital for the purpose of preserving ESOP value for participants and providing funds for the repurchase obligation. However, what the board decides to do in any given situation will depend on the facts presented. I am suggesting that when the facts are presented to the board, they need to look at them through different lenses. An approach that requires high growth may in fact be counterproductive if the share value increase leads to a crippling repurchase obligation.
6. *The board needs to understand the trustee's valuation process.* Under ERISA, the determination of annual share value is the trustee's decision. Notwithstanding this rule, the valuation has a direct impact on the corporation because of the repurchase obligation. The board must inform itself about the valuation process, and it must understand how valuation is affected by its decisions. A review of the company's valuation should be a regular feature of board governance.[27]

---

27. In ESOP purchase transactions, most professional trustees are loath to share the valuation work conducted by the trustee's financial advisor, even though there is no strict prohibition against sharing that information in the text of ERISA. Is this withholding of information helpful or harmful to the board of directors? Although it runs counter to much accepted wisdom, I argue that the withholding of this information, at least following the conclusion of the transaction, is not helpful at all. Instead, I argue that the board will better be able to serve the needs of all shareholders if it is briefed on the valuation report

The Duty of Loyalty

If the duty of care is designed to ensure that directors do not act stupidly, then the duty of loyalty is designed to make sure that directors do not act greedily and do not put their own interests above those of the shareholders. Most commonly, we think of the duty of loyalty as coming into play if directors favor themselves at the expense of the corporation in entering into contracts with the corporation or if they take business opportunities that otherwise should have belonged to the corporation. The duty of loyalty is also directly implicated whenever directors are also executives if they are approving compensation matters for themselves, leasing or purchasing real estate from an executive (typically the former majority shareholder), or establishing special executive bonus programs like stock appreciation rights plans.

For example, a board member may own a company that supplies a good or service to the corporation. (It could even be a lawyer who provides services to the corporation.) Whenever a board member is in that position, state law dictates that the board member can only act in the best interests of the corporation, not in his or her own interest (or in the interest of his or her other business). If a board member is involved in setting his or her own salary, again, the determination must be in the best interests of the corporation.

Determining whether potentially negligent board action involves a breach of the duty of loyalty rather than a breach of the duty of care is an important fundamental legal determination. If a case involves an allegation of a breach of a duty of care, then the burden of proof is on the plaintiff to show that the directors violated the duty, and the directors also can have the benefit of the business judgment rule as a defense for their actions. However, if a plaintiff alleges a breach of the duty of loyalty, then the burden of proof lies with the defendants (i.e., the board of directors), and there is no business judgment rule defense. Further, the courts have ruled that the business judgment rule does not apply to breaches of the duty of loyalty, and when the busi-

---

and becomes well versed in understanding the assumptions the ESOP trustee made in determining whether to purchase shares in the corporation.

ness judgment rule does not apply, the board's decisions must meet an "intrinsic fairness test."[28]

If there is a conflict of interest transaction that violates the duty of loyalty, the typical remedy is to unwind the transaction and force directors to give back whatever they have received. The earliest rules about conflict of interest transactions were actually quite simple: the rule was that corporations simply could not enter into conflict of interest transactions.

Modern corporate law statutes allow that conflict of interest transactions can be approved if a majority of disinterested directors approves, if a majority of disinterested shareholders approves, or if the transaction is fair. Court cases, however, seem to require that even if a transaction is approved by disinterested directors, it must also be fair.

A general rule that board members might bear in mind is that in conflict of interest lawsuits, the facts in the case will be disclosed in a way that is more likely to be unfavorable than the facts actually appeared to them. Also, it is useful for board members to consider that the most likely reason that a duty of loyalty case is brought is because there has been some level of corporate failure and disappointed shareholders are seeking to recover losses from the gains they perceive that certain interested parties received. Hence, when a conflict of interest transaction presents itself, boards should tread very carefully.

What Is Fairness?

A defense to a breach of loyalty allegation is that the involved transaction was "fair." A court review of fairness can involve a review of the end result of the decision, the process, or both.[29] The total question of fairness involves fair dealing and fair price. In other words, when a court reviews a conflict of interest transaction, the court asks "How would a stranger to the company have been treated in the negotiation (i.e., what would the process have been)?" and "What would the stranger have gotten for terms (i.e., what would the deal have been)?"

---

28. *Sinclair Oil Corp. v. Levien*, 280 A.2d 717 (Del. 1971).

29. *Weinberger v. UOP, Inc.*, 457 A.2d 701 (Del. 1983).

This sounds easy, but it is difficult for the courts to apply these rules because all transactions have fundamental differences. Plus, courts will implicitly be looking at transactions in hindsight, so boards must be able at some level to anticipate the likely economic results of the transaction.

For example, in an old case, a woolen mill owner was on the board of an electricity company. He received a contract that provided him with unlimited electricity at a cost equal to what he had been paying in prior years, following which he increased his usage dramatically. The court voided the contract because it said the board of directors of the electric company should have anticipated what would happen and that the electric company was harmed by the contract.[30]

Thus, although as a general rule fairness is measured at the time a transaction is entered into, later events can bear upon fairness. How is this so? If the later events are ones the directors should have anticipated or ones they did in fact anticipate, those later events will affect whether the court finds that the transaction was fair. The court's focus in looking at fairness usually ends up being a review of the substantive merits of the board's decision, and the key issue becomes candor. There can be no fairness without disclosure of the conflict of interest transaction.

There are some key areas in any closely held corporation where conflicts of interest become apparent, with one of the most frequent being compensation. In general, if there are interested parties involved in the compensation decision, boards will have to prove the fairness of the whole compensation package. Approval by disinterested shareholders will shift the burden of proof to the complainant to show how there is improper compensation. If disinterested directors approve, then the matter becomes subject to the business judgment rule. If there can be no disinterested approval (because there simply are no disinterested directors or shareholders), courts will look to Internal Revenue Service standards for reasonable compensation.[31]

---

30. *Globe Woolen Co. v. Utica Gas & Electric Co.*, 224 N.Y. 483, 121 N.E. 378 (1918).

31. *Wilderman v. Wilderman*, 315 A.2d 610 (Del. Ch. 1974).

Who Is Disinterested?

One of the issues that can be surprisingly challenging is whether in fact a director is disinterested. For example, in one case the spouse, father, and brother of an admittedly interested director were considered disinterested, while in another the interested director's attorney was considered not disinterested.[32] Under the Model Business Corporation Act, a director cannot have family, financial, professional, or an employment relationship with a person of such significance that one would reasonably expect a relationship to exert an influence on the judgment of the person in question and be considered disinterested.

Once the disinterested directors are determined, then the question becomes how many must vote on the transaction. Under Delaware law, a transaction can be approved by a majority of the disinterested directors, and a single disinterested director can approve a transaction. Under some state corporation laws, one needs a majority of the disinterested directors plus a majority of the quorum. The Model Business Corporation Act does not allow a single disinterested director to act. Further complicating the analysis is the fact that conflict of interest transactions can be approved after the fact even if the directors did not know that there was a conflict of interest transaction when the transaction was initially approved.

What about shareholder approval? Does shareholder approval repair everything? In general, the case law appears to say "no." Shareholders can vote according to their pocketbook issues. However, if the shareholders dominate the board of directors, then they may need to show that the transaction as a whole was fair.

If interested persons are both directors and shareholders, can they approve a conflict of interest transaction as shareholders that they could not otherwise approve as directors? The answer to this question also appears to be "no." Merely by changing hats, interested persons do not get some sort of special dispensation. If they are interested persons as directors, they are interested persons as shareholders. If it would be otherwise impossible for the vote to be passed, then they should understand the courts will apply a fairness review in determin-

32. Compare *Rocket Mining Corp. v. Jill*, 25 Utah 2nd 434, 43 P.2d 897 (1971), with *Sarner v. Fox Hill Gate, Inc.*, 151 Conn. 437, 199 A.2d 6 (1964).

ing whether the transaction can be approved, and they should seek an outside opinion as to whether the transaction or decision they made is fair.

Effect of the Failure to Disclose and What Must Be Disclosed

What if a conflict of interest has not been disclosed? Under some state laws, if there is failure to disclose any significant aspect of the conflict of interest, approval by disinterested directors or disinterested shareholders will be void. Some state statutes, however, provide that even if there is a failure to disclose, if fairness can be shown, then the transaction can go forward.

What must be disclosed? The general rule is easy to state but not so easy to apply—the interested parties must disclose all material facts that other directors would reasonably want to know. Unfortunately, one is not likely to know what facts should be considered material until after the fact, so broader disclosure makes more sense, and directors should exercise all discretion in favor of disclosure.

In truth, the effect of a failure to disclose or the inability to have disinterested persons approve a transaction is that the courts will review the decision under the rubric of fairness. If a court is using this review standard, it will essentially substitute its judgment for that of the board. In contrast, if a decision were subject to the business judgment rule, then a court will not (supposedly) substitute its judgment for the board's.

Implications of the Duty of Loyalty in the Context of Issues Common to ESOP Transactions

Whether or not recognized by board members, the duty of loyalty is frequently involved in transactions where an ESOP is buying part or all of the stock of a corporation and in decisions the board makes following the ESOP's acquisition of shares in the corporation. This happens most frequently in corporations where the board of directors is made up of key shareholders, managers, and their family members. What follows is a summary of some potential pitfalls and ideas on avoiding liability.

1. *Setting Compensation.* If board members are setting compensation for themselves as employees of the corporation, this is a classic conflict of interest. In an ESOP purchase transaction, an outside professional trustee will often review and comment on the level of compensation provided to key insiders. However, this is not a substitute for board action. The board must develop a system of assessing compensation standards for insiders. If the board is dominated by insiders, the use of an outside consultant in setting compensation, bonuses, and similar rights should be considered and in most cases used.
2. *Other Compensation Issues.* The board will also need to consider compensation being provided to family members of insiders. Are these family members being compensated for work actually performed, or is this a way of directing funds into the pockets of an owner's spouse or children? This type of transaction would be strictly reviewed by the courts.
3. *Lease Arrangements.* The board must review any leases of personal or real property with interested parties carefully. The best approach would be to obtain a third party appraisal to set a fair rate of rental, and the lease agreement itself should bear the hallmarks of a negotiated third party lease.
4. *The Seller's Future Role.* In many ESOP transactions, a selling shareholder's future role with the company will change either immediately following the transaction or some reasonable time thereafter. Perhaps the owner will be spending more time away from the business. The board must concern itself with how this seller will be compensated in the future; if his or her role is diminishing, the compensation should also diminish. The board must also concern itself with the perks provided to this shareholder and with the shareholder's formal stated role with the company.

The Business Judgment Rule

I now turn to a consideration of the business judgment rule. In its broadest form, a statement of the business judgment rule would give any board member great confidence that his or her actions are not likely to be challenged in court. Stated in its broadest sense, the business judgment rule "expresses the unanimous consent of American courts to eschew intervention in corporate decision-making if the judgment of directors and officers is uninfluenced by personal considerations and is exercised in good faith."[33] Stated slightly differently, the premises of the business judgment rule are that courts should not second-guess the business judgments of directors that have resulted nevertheless in poor results or with which reasonable minds might differ.[34] These expressions of the business judgment rule in turn raise the questions most frequently confronted by the courts: What is good faith? When will personal concerns be deemed to trump rational business concerns? What level of diligence must the board engage in? In addition, this statement of the business judgment rule makes one wonder how any board gets sued for its actions. The reason is, as I shall discuss, that the descriptions of the business judgment rule are too broad and likely give false comfort to members of boards of directors.

The business judgment rule on its face only applies to decisions the board makes; it does not, in other words, provide a defense for lack of attention. Moreover, the rule is not absolute. Rather, it creates a presumption. If a board decision lies within the realm of the business judgment rule (i.e., it is not tainted by self-interest), then it is up to the plaintiff to demonstrate that the board did not act in good faith or with due care.[35]

So what kinds of actions end up falling outside of the business judgment rule? It is hard to generalize, because each case is fact-specific. In one example, a board was found liable when it authorized the corporation to buy debentures where the seller was given price protection (it could buy back the debentures if their value increased at the price the seller sold the debentures), but the buyer did not get price protection

33. *Miller v. American Telephone and Telegraph Co.*, 507 F.2d 759, 762 (3d. Cir. 1974).

34. Franklin Gevurtz, *Corporation Law* (St. Paul, MN: West, 2000), 278–79. See also *Litwin v. Allen*, 25 N.Y.S.2d 667, 678 (Sup. Ct. 1940) ("[D]irectors are liable for negligence in the performance of their duties . . . [they] are not liable for errors of judgment or for mistakes while acting with reasonable skill and prudence.").

35. See *Aronson v. Lewis*, 473 A.2d 805 (Del. 1984).

(i.e., to be able to sell back at the issue price if the value decreased).[36] In another case, a board's decision to spin off a losing division was deemed a protected decision even though the plaintiffs alleged that a sale of the business would have generated helpful tax losses.[37]

Smith v. Van Gorkum,[38] a Delaware case, is one of the seminal business judgment rule cases and serves as a useful tool for understanding the business judgment rule in a real-world application. In the case, Mr. Van Gorkum, the CEO of Trans Union Corporation, negotiated a deal to sell Trans Union for $55 a share in cash to a company controlled by Jay Pritzker in a merger. By state law the merger had to be approved by the directors and then voted upon and approved by the shareholders of Trans Union.

The court ruled that the directors were liable for approving this transaction. In making this ruling, the court emphasized that the board approved the transaction after only a two-hour meeting during which Mr. Van Gorkum made a 20-minute oral presentation about the transaction. There were no handouts, and the board did not review the merger documents or inquire into how the price was arrived at. The price, however, represented a premium over its previous $38 per share trading price.

A dissent argued that the *Van Gorkum* decision was essentially creating a form of strict liability for directors; notably, the board was composed of skilled business people, including CEOs of other large corporations and a former dean of the University of Chicago School of Business. The majority, however, determined that the process the board used was flawed. It was too cursory, notwithstanding the skills and experience of the board.

This is the important lesson of the *Van Gorkum* case. The business judgment rule will protect a board when it has the right processes in place; if the board is composed of well-seasoned business minds but

---

36. See *Litwin v. Allen*.

37. *Kamin v. American Express Company*, 86 Misc. 2d 809, 383 N.Y.S. 2d 807 (1976).

38. 488 A.2d 858 (Del. 1985). For the purpose of full disclosure, I will note that I clerked for the author of that opinion, Justice Henry R. Horsey, from 1988 to 1989.

does not adopt a good process, then the board's decisions will not necessarily be protected by the business judgment rule.

When does the formation of good processes begin? It begins long before a merger agreement is negotiated and long before any other significant decisions are made. It begins in the day-to-day activities of the board, with the board identifying the core aspects of the business that require the board's regular review and monitoring; it begins with the board establishing committees and other tools by which the board informs itself of key decision-making processes and determinations of the management team; and it begins with the board taking an inquisitive—but not inquisitorial—approach to the company. The board must be interested; it must be a curious learner about what is going on with the company's business.

These concepts are supported by the New York case of *Auerbach v. Bennett.*[39] In this case, shareholders of GTE sought to bring what is known as a "derivative" lawsuit on behalf of the company against its directors and outside accountants in connection with certain suspicious payments to overseas political officials and parties. In a derivative suit, plaintiffs seek essentially to take away from the board the ability to determine whether the company should initiate a lawsuit or not. Under state law, the board is entitled to investigate the wisdom of commencing the suit.

So, in *Auerbach,* in response to the plaintiff's suit, the board created a special committee of directors who were not accused of wrongdoing to review the claim in order to determine whether to recommend that the corporation go forward with the lawsuit. The committee, after extensive review, declined to do so, and the court ruled that the business judgment rule protected this decision and that the plaintiff's suit should be dismissed.

In making this ruling, the court determined that the only aspect of the committee's decision that was subject to review was the process it used in determining not to go forward. If the process was fair, then the substantive decision of the committee would be upheld under the business judgment rule. So, once the court determined that the process was fair, it declined to review the substantive decision.

---

39. 47 N.Y.2d 619, 393 N.E.2d 994, 419 N.Y.S.2d 920 (1979).

The Application of the Business Judgment Rule in the Sale of Business Setting

We have seen how the business judgment rule may be thought of as a rule of conduct governing processes of boards. A little bit later I will explore how following some of the principles of Sarbanes-Oxley and establishing board committees may lend themselves to creating a business judgment shield for key decisions by the board. But before turning to those topics, I shall review the application of the business judgment rule in the specific context of a sale of the company.

During the decades of the 1980s and 1990s, business takeover contests were gold mines for court decisions delineating how a board should respond to unsolicited takeover proposals. These decisions are particularly of interest to ESOP companies that wish to remain independent and ESOP-owned but also are worried about the board fiduciary issues that might arise from a takeover defense that is comprised of "just say no."

What Are Takeover Defenses?

Determining how takeover defenses will be reviewed by courts is important to ESOP companies that desire to remain ESOP-owned and prevent an unwanted third-party takeover. Typical plain vanilla takeover defenses include the following: (1) having staggered terms for directors, (2) requiring supermajority votes for sale transactions, and (3) having provisions that change the voting rights of stock if a certain percentage of the stock is acquired by an outsider. Each of the foregoing defenses involves a change to the company's articles of incorporation and requires a shareholder vote. For example, in *Williams v. Geier,*[40] the corporation's articles had a provision under which the corporation's shares lost voting power if they were transferred. They would regain voting power if the buyer retained the shares for three years. The court determined that this defense was acceptable.

A more esoteric defense is the "poison pill," of which there are a number of variations. In one typical poison pill, the company issues convertible preferred stock to its common stockholders. This stock

---

40. See *Williams v. Geier*, 671 A.2d 1368 (Del. 1996).

contains a curious right: if another company buys a certain amount of the issuer's stock and then merges with the buyer, the convertible preferred stock gives the target's shareholders the right to convert into the buyer's stock at a favorable rate. The board retains the right to redeem the convertible preferred if it chooses.

Another form of poison pill enables the holders of the convertible preferred to force a redemption of the poison pill at a high price, making the target company less valuable. Still another form is issued as convertible debt with a restriction on the target company's ability to incur more debt (which presumably a buyer would need to do in order to acquire the firm). Unlike the plain vanilla takeover defenses cited above, a board of directors can generally adopt, distribute, and redeem poison pills without resorting to shareholder approval.

How Are Takeover Defenses Reviewed?

Unless a management buyout is implicated, takeover defenses should not implicate the duty of loyalty and conflict of interest analysis. If a company adopts a takeover defense and has it approved by its shareholders, it is possible that the decision is fully protected and cannot be challenged.[41]

If a board takes steps to prevent a takeover in response to a takeover threat, the analysis shifts. In that instance, the board must be able to show that the proposed takeover represents a threat to the corporate policy and that the steps taken are reasonable in relationship to the threat.[42] Once the board determines, however, that a sale is inevitable, then its sole acceptable goal is to obtain the highest price,[43] but only if the board decides to engage in a bid process. If the board does not engage in a bid process, it does not have to commence an auction.

---

41. *Mills Acquisition Co. v. Macmillan, Inc.*, 559 A.2d 1261 (Del. 1989).
42. *Unocal Corp. v. Mesa Acquisition Co.*, 413 A.2d 946 (Del. 1985).
43. *Revlon, Inc. v. MacAndrews & Forbes Holdings, Inc.*, 506 A.2d 173 (Del. 1985).

State Anti-takeover Statutes

In response to the takeover craze and the concomitant loss of local jobs, many states enacted corporate legislation that was designed to slow down the progress of takeovers of public companies. One type of statute required a shareholder vote in order to allow the purchasing shareholder to vote its shares. The purpose of this kind of statute was to place tender offers on a playing field that was substantially similar to merger transactions (which require board and shareholder approval). The U.S. Supreme Court denied a constitutional challenge to this kind of provision in *CTS Corp. v. Dynamics Corp. of America*.[44] I will discuss some ideas associated with this kind of statute a little later.

The Impact of Sarbanes-Oxley

Boards of directors of ESOP companies should consider the application of Sarbanes-Oxley. By its wording the statute only applies to publicly traded companies, but some of its principles are worth considering in the ESOP setting.

Sarbanes-Oxley arose largely out of the debacles caused by the implosion of Enron and several other companies that were seen largely to relate to a lack of financial oversight by boards of directors. A key aspect of the law is that the corporate board of a publicly traded company must have an independent audit committee to oversee the audit of the books of the company, and the auditor must report directly to the committee without the intervention of the company's executive officers. The audit committee must also include at least one person who actually understands financial reporting.

In addition, Sarbanes-Oxley requires that the CEO and CFO of the company must personally certify the accuracy of the financial statements of the company and that management of the company establish effective internal controls. A consideration of Sarbanes-Oxley can be especially helpful when the board of an ESOP company considers establishing committees.

---

44. 481 U.S. 69, 107 S. Ct. 1637 (1987).

Why Establishing and Using Board Committees Is Essential for Any Board

I noted earlier that state corporation statues permit the board to establish committees to perform certain functions of the board other than, in general, declaring dividends, voting to amend the corporate charter, or voting to sell or merge the company. If they are properly constructed and used, board committees can enable the board to fulfill its duties in such a way as to make the favorable application of the business judgment rule more likely. Well-run board committees should also help the management of the corporation operate more smoothly.

Committees are generally formed in one of two ways. First, they may be mandated by the bylaws of the corporation, and the bylaws may set out in detail the operations of the committees. Second, a company's bylaws may provide that the board has the power to create standing (i.e., permanent) and ad hoc committees and to provide how the committees shall be staffed and how they shall operate. In this second instance, the charter of the committee is set forth by the board when it creates the committee.

Some other general principles can be described for effective committees. First, the committees should be composed of no more than three to five directors and should have a clear written mandate approved by the board as a whole. If a committee is a standing committee, the board should set term limits so that all members of the board can have an opportunity to serve and so that one committee does not predominate over time. The staff reporting and support requirements for the committee should be clearly established so that the committee members will know whom they are to rely on for reports and other information.

In an ESOP company, the most typical board committees are (1) the audit/finance committee; (2) the ESOP committee; (3) the board succession committee; and (4) the management succession committee. Each of these committees may have different names in a given company, and the precise roles of the committees vary from company to company. In the discussion that follows, the allocation of responsibilities among committees is generally not legally required. However, I would argue that the creation of an audit/finance committee along the lines I will describe is essential for a board that desires the protection of the business judgment rule.

The audit/finance committee will oversee the company's annual budgeting process, review the monthly or quarterly financial reports of the company, review the performance of the company's chief financial officer, and meet independently with the company's auditor. The audit/finance committee should also review and approve the projections supplied each year by management to the ESOP trustee and its valuation firm.

The ESOP committee may play several roles. First, if the company has a separate ESOP committee staffed by employees that functions either as a fiduciary of the ESOP or as communication committee for the ESOP, then the board ESOP committee will interface with that other ESOP committee on a regular basis. The board ESOP committee shall also educate itself and the board about the ESOP on a regular basis and ensure that the board as a whole understands the operation and importance of the ESOP to the employees and the company. The board ESOP committee should also serve as the first level of review of any changes proposed to the ESOP document. The role of a board ESOP committee may be subsumed within the activities of a board human resource committee that oversees employee benefits and general employee relations at the company.

In addition to the foregoing, the ESOP committee may also serve as the primary conduit for communication between the ESOP trustee and the board. The ESOP committee may take an active role with the trustee and the employee ESOP committee in communicating the annual valuation and other important ESOP milestones to employees.

The board succession committee would meet on a less frequent basis than other board committees. Its primary responsibility would be to develop lists of successors to the board as vacancies arose. One of the mandates of this committee would be to ensure that new board members quickly share in and appreciate the impetus that created the ESOP and employee ownership at the company.

The management succession committee would meet on a regular basis to assess with the CEO the performance of key management personnel and to develop an ongoing succession plan for all levels of employees throughout the company. This committee could also take on the role of the CEO's succession planning. One interesting approach that the committee might take is to develop a deferred compensation plan for the CEO that vests only once he or she has nominated and successfully put in place his or her successor.

Larger boards of directors will also want to consider creating an executive committee to handle matters the full board would handle in between its regular meetings. Other committees may be formed on an ad hoc basis for such things as site searches if the business is looking to expand or move. In addition, the board may want to establish a standing committee whose only role is to review any outside bids for the acquisition of the business.

Boards, Outside Board Members, and the Oversight of Management—What Is Involved?

Now that I have reviewed the various duties of a board of directors and discussed the potential composition of board committees, it is appropriate to provide a review of how a board should exercise its duties in overseeing management and to explore whether companies with ESOPs should have outside board members.

By "outside," I mean that the board member is neither an employee of the company nor a contractor (i.e., lawyer, accountant, or other professional) to the company. The emerging trend is clearly that companies with ESOPs, especially with majority ESOP ownership, should bring in outside board members. Another emerging trend is that outside board members will form a majority of the members of the board audit/finance committee.

What are the reasons for these trends? First, while it is still not uncommon to find companies where executives are also board members and trustees (sometimes wearing all three hats), there is a growing recognition that outsiders bring an important attribute of independence and will also ask questions where others either would not think to do so or simply not see the reason to ask the questions.

The outside board members can also serve the vital role of reviewing and approving compensation for the CEO and other key executives. Whether as a permanent or ad hoc committee, if outside board members make a careful assessment and approval of executive compensation (include stock appreciation rights plans), that determination is subject to review under the business judgment rule. If insiders perform that review, then the determination is subject to the much stricter conflict of interest analysis.[45]

The introduction of outside board members is, in my view, essential to the healthy functioning of an ESOP-owned company. Under ERISA and state corporate law there is an unbroken circle—the board appoints the trustee, and the ESOP appoints the board. If there is too tight a confluence between the board members and the trustee, there is simply no way of introducing new ideas into the management of the corporation. Without the introduction of outside board members, I would argue that every decision made by the board is subject to conflict of interest analysis and therefore overturns the defense of the business judgment rule for the board.

In many cases, owners and management resist the idea of outside board directors out of a fear that board members (1) will interfere too much with the operations of a corporation and (2) will understand too little about the operations of the company. There is also often an assumption, stated and unstated, that outside board members will be antagonistic toward management. None of these assumptions is necessarily accurate, and, with appropriate care and feeding, it is more likely that a working relationship between the board and the key officers can develop that supports the executives and the company over time.

How might this happen? First, the board must clearly view itself as *not* being a micro-manager, and management can reinforce this conclusion by doing the micromanagement well. Second, the company should have a clear corporate mission and clear short-term, mid-term, and long-term goals against which the board can assess results. The board should be involved in setting these goals. Third, the board should view itself as supporting management through careful questioning and evaluation. If the board feels management is losing its way, it should point this out soon but also be able to offer insights as to how to move

45. In addition, if a committee of outside board directors approved such compensation packages and demonstrated prudence in the process of review and approval, it is likely that the Department of Labor would be less inclined to look at such programs unfavorably from an ERISA perspective.

forward. Finally, the board itself should honestly self-evaluate itself and its actions on a regular basis.

These actions all should take place within the context of the committee structures I outlined earlier. When a board is first embarking on creating these committees and making them functioning entities, it may be necessary to obtain some outside consulting help. However, within two to three years, the board should be able to function at a high level on its own. The use of consultants after that period of time could be appropriately limited to bringing in a facilitator for annual board retreats and for particularly sticky issues.

In the day-to-day (more likely quarter-to-quarter) functions of the board, the use of committees will be essential, and the board would do well to consider carefully how information shall flow to and from it as it exercises these duties.

The most important board relationship is between the board and the CEO. The board or the executive committee should meet in person or by phone with the CEO on a regular basis, at least quarterly, and more frequently if circumstances require. I believe that the board's primary role is not to critique the CEO's actions but to support them. At the same time, the board must maintain a delicate balancing act of calling the CEO to task if he or she is not performing his or her duties. The decision of whether to fire the CEO is best seen as a decision of last resort. Boards should desire that the CEO be a strong leader who does not feel that he or she is always being second-guessed.

The role of the audit/finance committee cannot be understated. Members of the committee should receive clear monthly reports by email showing the company's performance at least against the prior year's period and against projections. The committee should meet in person or by phone at least quarterly. If the committee does not feel the information it is receiving is reliable or acceptable, it must work immediately with the chief financial officer (or controller or finance director) to get the information it wants. If the problem persists, then the committee should report this to either the chair of the board or the CEO.

Board committees may also interface directly with other aspects of the corporation's business. Many companies have human resources committees that deal with salary and benefit issues. In an ESOP company, this committee should be rolled into the ESOP committee I have previously described. This committee should meet on at least a quarterly basis with the director of human resources (or the person functionally holding that role) and should evaluate the work performed by that team leader. If the committee does not feel the information it is receiving is reliable or acceptable, it must work immediately with the human resource director to get the information it wants. If the problem persists, the committee should report this to either the chair of the board or the CEO.

Board Duties When the ESOP Adoption and a Sale to an ESOP Is Considered

I will now turn to an examination of the board's roles and functions when a company is first considering the creation of an ESOP and a transaction with an ESOP. I will point out that much of what follows comes from my personal experience not only in working with companies establishing ESOPs but also in talking and working with other lawyers who were advising their clients about an ESOP or ESOP transaction.

I think that a metaphor is useful here. I like to think that the establishment of an ESOP and the implementation of ESOP transaction is a river, even though to most clients, when the paperwork starts flowing, it feels more like a flood. This river is wide and deep and derives its power from many tributaries, and each of these tributaries is, in and of itself, its own important and self-sustaining ecosystem. In the consideration of the ESOP and the ESOP transaction, I think the following are the main tributaries of which the board needs to be aware.

The ESOP Plan Document Itself

The board ultimately approves the plan documents that create the ESOP. The board must decide what choices should be made about, among other things, participation and vesting, about crediting prior years of service and about distributions, and about beneficiary voting rights.[46] In reviewing the choices for the plan document the board has

46. I want to thank and acknowledge Alex Moss of Praxis Consulting for the ideas I present here in the consideration of the ESOP plan document. These

enormous leeway. Determining the plan document terms is a settlor function and is not subject to review under ERISA.

I suggest the board establish a committee consisting of board members and employees to craft the plan document with the assistance of an outside advisor. In making decisions, the board should become mindful of how certain decisions such as vesting and crediting prior service can affect the repurchase obligation of the company and can affect how employees will view the plan and make decisions appropriately. If the board does this right, the outcomes will be better plan design decisions, better employee buy-in (understanding and acceptance) due to better engagement up front, and clarity around decision-making principles. What is most important is that the plan structure be adopted mindfully. The board should be informed about what decisions may affect not only the company's finances but also the utility of the ESOP as an employee motivational tool.

In creating a committee to review the ESOP plan document, the board should identify: the overall objectives of the group reviewing the plan design; the specific ESOP issues for consideration; the constraints, i.e., what is not on the table for the group to consider (for example, the board may state that immediate vesting of all employees is not an option); decision-making parameters—should the plan design committee make recommendations or have final authority; and criteria and selection process for persons to become members of the design team.

The key decisions for the committee to review and the board to approve are the following:

- Eligibility, participation, and vesting
- How contributions will be made (i.e., though employer contributions or dividends and distributions on shares)
- How stock will be voted and on what issues (other than as legally required) participants shall be entitled to vote
- Distribution policies

---

concepts are derived from presentations Alex and I have made for the National Center for Employee Ownership, the Vermont Employee Ownership Center, and others.

In making decisions about these issues, the board should focus on some general principles as well, such as how certain decisions will act as incentives or disincentives to employees (both current and future employees), how employees will perceive the decision-making process surrounding the ESOP's creation, and what cost considerations are associated with certain decisions.

The Transaction Structure

The financing and structuring of ESOP transactions can be complex and will affect a company's finances for years to come. A well-planned ESOP transaction will include a careful "before and after" analysis of the impact of the transaction on the company's finances, including its income statements and balance sheet and, if required, its bonding requirements.

The board should consider engaging an outside advisor to propose and assess various transaction structures. The board's role in reviewing the transaction should be consistent with the way it would view any other financing or stock sale transaction. The board must assess the impact of the transaction on the long-term needs of the company. It must determine whether the transaction best suits the company.

One issue that frequently arises is the question of how much employees need to know about the transaction. An owner is often concerned with whether employees have to know what he or she received in the transaction. The board is not legally obligated to disclose the financial details of a transaction to employees; however, the interests of having a broadly inclusive structure indicate that reasonable disclosure of the deal is better over the long run. For example, let us say in an ESOP transaction an owner or group of owners is to receive $5 million that is borrowed from a bank and will be paid back over five years. The participants in the ESOP will have a much better sense of what their task is (work hard to pay off a $5 million loan) if they have an understanding of the transaction. Furthermore, having a concrete goal (paying off the $5 million loan) can be useful in building the camaraderie of the company. With proper education, most employees will recognize that the owner deserves to receive payment for his or her shares and will welcome the opportunity to be the buyer through the

ESOP rather than to be an employee of a new unknown third-party buyer.

In assessing whether to engage in the transaction, the board should establish an ad hoc committee or use its existing finance committee to work with the company's chief financial officer and outside advisors in modeling the transaction. In this modeling, the board should assess how the transaction will affect the company and how it is projected to perform and pay off the debt that will be incurred in the transaction. The board should also examine how a downturn in the business might affect the transaction as well.

Separately from the board's review of the transaction structure, the ESOP trustee must also approve the transaction. The board cannot simply rely on the fact that the ESOP trustee has approved the transaction; it must make an independent determination that the transaction is in the best interests of the company. The *Smith v. Van Gorkum* case described earlier tells us that the board cannot make this decision in a single meeting. Instead the board must deliberate about the transaction over time and receive analysis about the transaction. The board must also receive presentations about the transaction documents and understand precisely what is happening in the transaction. Again, establishing an ad hoc committee to perform some of this work would be an appropriate exercise of the board's fiduciary function.

Communicating the ESOP Plan and Transaction to Employees

ESOPs work best as motivational tools when employees know and understand the operation of the ESOP and how they can benefit over time from the transaction. Part of implementing an ESOP structure is also creating an educational program to help employees understand the ESOP and to encourage them to learn to act as owners.

The board can initiate this process in the plan design stage by incorporating employee participation into the board processes associated with adopting the ESOP. In connection with the adoption of the ESOP, the board should direct that management create an ESOP committee for employees, the purposes of which will include to learn about the ESOP and to be able to communicate the ESOP to employees. The board (or its ESOP committee) should receive regular reports from the ESOP communication committee.

Creating Appropriate Incentives for Management

The implementation of an ESOP, especially where a company is becoming 100% ESOP-owned or plans to become 100% ESOP-owned, will make the idea of compensating upper management with stock options or similar equity based programs, including the flat-out issuance of stock, mostly obsolete. This is because the tax savings from ESOP ownership in S corporations are likely to become too good to pass up, and the board will determine that having any outside non-ESOP ownership is not in the best interests of the company. Further, the tax savings enjoyed by 100% ESOP-owned S corporations will make financing and structuring transactions easier because the money that would otherwise go to taxes can be used to pay off financing.

Managers will enjoy equity participation through the ESOP, but in general boards will also want to consider how to create further incentives through such programs as stock appreciation rights plans for management. Many independent ESOP trustees will also want such programs in place to create structures to attract highly skilled management to the company.

The board will want to start reviewing these issues as soon as it is beginning to consider the ESOP at any serious level. This work may be devolved to the finance committee or to the management succession committee. The key questions the board needs to focus on are what incentives will work and how the structure will affect the company. Within this context the board will have to decide how much "phantom" equity will be set aside for management; what members of management will be eligible to participate in the plan; how managers will vest in the plan (will it just happen over time or will the company have to meet certain targets for vesting to occur?); and whether the issuance of such rights will be conditioned on the manager entering into some kind on non-competition agreement.

An equity incentive program will also create a debit on the company's balance sheet and may affect the company's ability to borrow or bond, so the board will have to consider these issues as well. The board's decisions on these issues will affect the ESOP, as any equity incentive will be dilutive of the ESOP's ownership; accordingly, the board must also get the buy-in of the incentive structure from the ESOP trustee.

In making these decisions, the board will also have to be aware of the conflict of interest rules. If all the board members are going to participate in the stock appreciation rights plan, the board's decision to establish the plan and its decisions about the design of the plan will be subject to strict scrutiny by the courts. If outside directors were present and independently approved of the plan, however, their decision would be subject to the business judgment rule.

Developing a Board Structure That Is Supportive of ESOP Culture

Most closely held corporations have board structures wherein the key shareholders are also the board members and the officers of the company. It is my belief that such a structure does not work well over the long haul for an ESOP company and that part of the board's long-term planning is to replace that structure with ones that are suggested in this chapter.

In an ideal world, the appointment of outside board members and the creation of a board audit/finance committee, a majority of which would be outside board members, would occur before the ESOP is adopted and the transaction takes place. I recognize that this ideal is simply not likely to happen. However, hopefully one can see how beneficial it would be to have outsiders review the adoption of the ESOP, the transaction structure, and management compensation issues.

Might there be an alternative for a company that is choosing, as by far the majority do, to deal with board issues after the transaction? I think there is. A solution may be to create an informal board of advisors composed of two to four businesspeople whose companies have experienced ESOP transactions. This group might meet informally three or four times to give the current owners advice about all of the foregoing issues.

In connection with this revitalizing of the board, I believe that there should also be a commitment in writing that the board members will be educated about the ESOP and that an understanding of the ESOP and the culture imbued in the ESOP must be attained by all board members. As part of this, the board will commit to a regular program of education for new and old board members.

Inside the Purchase and Sale Agreement: Board Considerations

The agreements relating to the ESOP purchase and sale transaction require the direct attention of and consideration by the board. The board cannot simply rubber-stamp the documents presented to it. The board, of course, will need to understand the financial implications of the transaction and whether the company can handle taking on the debt required by the transaction. But the board must also undertake to understand the more mundane aspects of the transaction.

In particular, the board should take care to review what representations and warranties the company is making in the purchase and sale documents to the ESOP buyer and to any lenders and what level of indemnification the company is giving the ESOP buyer and to lenders. This review is required as a matter of the board's prudent exercise of the duty of care because the corporation cannot make these representations unless the board authorizes it to. As a matter of law, the board authorizes these representations and warranties when it makes resolutions approving the transactions associated with the ESOP purchase.

As part of the board's review of deal documents, it should receive an overview of the company's representations and warranties. This will consist of a laundry list of items including that the company has paid its taxes on a timely basis; that the company's financial statements are accurate; that the company is not under investigation for any wrongdoing; and that the company is not in violation of any environmental laws. The board may designate the responsibility to undertake this review to an ad hoc committee. The board's role is to make sure that it is comfortable with the company making the representations, and the board may wish to ask for company officers to sign certifications about certain representations. For example, it may want the chief financial officer to sign a Sarbanes-Oxley style certification about the company's financials.

The board also has to undertake a review of any significant contracts beyond the purchase and sale agreement, such as leases with related parties and employment agreements. The board also must review the terms of all financing arrangements incurred in the transaction with any lending institution and any sellers (i.e., through seller notes). The board's role here is to ensure that the company is, in short, getting a reasonable deal. The board's perception of itself in these actions should be that of a careful overseer of the fortunes of the company. The board in this matter is representing the company and must determine whether, as a whole, the transaction will be fair to the company.

Some questions a board should wonder about are: How far into the future must the board prognosticate? How deep should a board get on such issues as repurchase obligation? Does a truly independent board require separate legal representation? There are no simple answers to these questions, but some rules of thumb may be helpful.

As to projections, I think anything beyond five years is entirely guesswork, so there should be no obligation to go beyond that. Projections of three to five years should be adequate, but the board should revisit such projections on at least an annual basis after the transaction is done.

I believe boards should always be looking at the repurchase obligation. The only question is what level of study should be done. If a company has had an ESOP for a long period of time and is going from minority to majority ownership (for instance from 35% ownership to 100%), it should get a repurchase study performed. If the transaction is a minority transaction that will be financed over time, a full-blown study is not generally necessary before the transaction, but it should be performed as more and more employees become vested. If a company stock redemption is occurring in connection with the transaction, the board should inquire as to how that redemption structure will affect the repurchase obligation, if at all.

What about separate legal representation? In general this should not be necessary, in that the company's counsel serves the wishes of the majority of the board of directors. However, if a transaction is complex and if the independent outside board members are being asked to vote separately on the transaction because of conflict of interest concerns, then I believe that a good argument can be made that having separate

ESOP counsel to advise these board members would serve to create a more independent process and one more likely to enjoy the shield of the business judgment rule.

Non-Alignment of Shareholders' Interests When ESOP Is a Minority

We have seen earlier how, in a closely held corporation, the members of the board of directors are usually the key shareholders and the key officers of the company. In fact, these director/officer/shareholder owners generally view themselves more as partners in the enterprise than as passive investors.

The introduction of the ESOP as a minority shareholder changes this calculus. The ESOP and the other owners certainly share common interests and goals, such as growing the business and maintaining and growing a profitable enterprise. The employees indirectly represented through the ESOP are also aligned with the original owners' interests.

This alignment, however, is not perfect; what follows then is a non-exhaustive list of what might be called "issues of non-alignment." By thinking through these issues, members of a board of directors of a minority-owned ESOP company can begin to appreciate the change that should come with the introduction of the ESOP.

1. *The ESOP is a passive owner.* Before the ESOP transaction, all owners in the closely held enterprise are likely to have been "active," i.e., working and managing the business. The ESOP, regardless of whether the trustee is an institution or an individual or group of individuals, is not active. It simply cannot be, because it is an entity, not a human being. Moreover, the ESOP trustee is holding the stock on behalf of another and is subject to a panoply of rules under ERISA that govern its conduct.
2. *The ESOP shareholder is really a number of very different shareholders.* The ESOP trustee represents a group of persons that ranges from the key officers of the company to the lowest-paid worker and from persons a year from retirement to persons decades from retirement. The interests of these persons can vary widely and in quite surprising ways.

Consider the following example. Suppose a minority-owned ESOP company is located in a relatively rural area and its chief financial officer makes $150,000 a year and is 55 years old. There are no comparable CFO jobs within 200 miles that would pay the same. Let us further assume that a driver for the company earns $20 an hour and that is the going rate for drivers in the area and there are plenty of openings for experienced drivers in the area. How would each of these individuals respond to different business decisions, such as taking a risky plunge into a new business line or a sale? They should respond quite differently, with the CFO being much more conservative than the driver. But how can the board represent these different interests, especially if there is no voice for the different interests on the board?

3. *The ESOP may be more of an "investor" than a "worker."* An ESOP is a retirement plan as well as a financing vehicle to provide for orderly ownership transitions. Court cases have generally indicated that the ESOP is a "special" retirement plan. Thus, the ESOP trustee is permitted to invest primarily in employer stock, even though that decision concentrates the assets of the trust in one specific investment.[47] Even so, the ESOP trust by its nature focuses more on the preservation and reasonable growth of capital. Accordingly, its interests may be different from those of the original founder shareholders.

The 100% ESOP Transaction: Special Considerations

I believe there are special considerations for boards of companies that are considering 100% ESOP ownership transactions, whether the company is going from partial or zero ESOP ownership to 100%. Further, these considerations may be slightly different for the partially ESOP owned company than for the company going from zero ESOP ownership to 100%.

---

47. See, e.g., *Moench v. Robertson*, 62 F.3d 553 (3rd Cir. 1993); *In re McKesson HBOC, Inc. ERISA Litigation*, 391 F. Supp. 2d 812 (N.D. Cal. 2005).

The Partially Owned ESOP Company

A board in a partially owned ESOP company must consider whether the fiduciary rules of ERISA are implicated in the decisions the board makes. Although as a general rule ERISA does not regulate the business judgments of the board, the board must take care to ensure that it is not functioning as the trustee of the ESOP when it is making decisions.

Avoiding this should be relatively easy. First, the board must determine whether it has reserved for itself the right to direct the trustee of the ESOP concerning its fiduciary function. If it has, the board needs to relinquish that right and to appoint an independent trustee to consider all facets of the second-stage ESOP transaction.

The board will also want to consider the impact of the second stage on the value of shares already held in the ESOP. In most instances the ESOP trustee will want to negotiate "price protection" for participants in the ESOP who die, become disabled, or take normal retirement for some period following the second-stage transaction. In negotiating this protection, the board should consult with the company's financial advisors about the appropriate term of such protection. Typically, the price protection lasts for a period of years and guarantees a share price for distribution purposes for persons in the protected class that is determined by excluding the impact of the second-stage transaction.

If the board has not moved toward a more formalized board structure with committees and outside members, it should do so as part of the second-stage transaction. The board should also undertake a repurchase obligation study to determine whether or not a given transaction structure will result in a more easily absorbed repurchase obligation for the company.

The Zero to 100% Transaction

The board's duties in the zero to 100% transaction are heightened, in my view, because it will be nearly impossible for the company to undo the transaction except through a sale to a third party. The board must carefully consider why it wants to make the decision and what it hopes to accomplish. The board must further make a commitment to employee involvement in the company if it wants the company to enjoy the ESOP performance advantage. Establishing some kind of advisory board with executives and former owners of other 100% ESOP-owned companies to assist in the transition is an alternative such companies should consider.

Issues Common to Both Kinds of Transactions

Most single and second-stage 100% ESOP transactions will involve significant seller financing that is accompanied with the issuance of warrants.[48] The ESOP trustee will review that financing to determine whether the terms are fair to the ESOP. The board needs to review the terms of such financing for its essential fairness to the company. Issues the board should consider are whether the terms of the seller notes and warrants taken as a whole are reasonable given other financing that may be available to the company; whether the terms of the warrants along with any other equity schemes may violate Section 409(p) of the Internal Revenue Code (the "Code"); and how the terms of the warrant payoffs may impact the company in the future. A regular review of the status of the warrants should become a staple of the board's financial oversight of the company.

When the company becomes 100% ESOP-owned, the so-called "multiple hat" problem will also be more apparent. By this, I mean that if the same persons are officers, directors, and ESOP trustees, the role an individual is playing in a given circumstance will often be unclear. For example, an officer's duty can broadly be conceived as being to commit capital to grow the business and to take appropriate risks in doing so; in opposition, an ESOP trustee's duty can be viewed as being to conserve capital to ensure that a participant's retirement is secured. These duties necessarily conflict.

It is my belief that any company that is 100% ESOP-owned should move—even if it takes a few years—to having a board that is predominantly made up of outside members. Even so, this board must be committed to the company's ESOP ownership structure while also serving as an engaged monitor of the performance of the company's executives. The movement toward this kind of structure

48. James G. Steiker, "Warrants in ESOP Transactions," *Journal of Employee Ownership Law and Finance*, vol. 20, no. 2 (spring 2008): 107.

should be acknowledged as part of the single or second-stage 100% ESOP transaction, and steps toward that structure should be initiated as part of that transaction.

In looking at the second-stage or 100% transaction, the board must consider how the transaction will affect executives who might otherwise have thought they would have received equity in the company either through a direct issuance of stock, through options, or through any other kind of purchase. Will these executives accept or resent the ESOP? Can they work constructively within the framework of an ESOP, or is an ESOP company just not right for them? The board should engage in a deliberate process of interviewing key executives to make sure that they want the transaction to happen. Indeed, the board may want to give them the option of trying to finance their own buyout of the company.

If the company has a stock appreciation rights plan in place, the board will want to consider how the ESOP transaction will affect that plan. Some sort of price protection for the plan may be in order, but care must be given to the question of whether such protection might violate the one-class-of-stock rule for S corporations and of how the price protection would affect Section 409(p) testing. A better alternative might be to adopt a new plan and issue more units or replacement units for the old plan.

The board must also assess how the second-stage or 100% transaction may affect the company's ability to access capital for growth and other purposes and the company's ability to obtain surety bonds. For construction firms in particular, the sureties should be part of the discussion from day one. It is vitally important that the bond issuers themselves are involved, not just the agents.

In all of this, what I hope is apparent is that procedural prudence is the touchstone to success. The board needs actively to consider the issues I have outlined, and its review of the issues needs to be documented. If there already are outside board directors, the process will legally be a better process. If no outside board members exist, the board needs to perform its work knowing that legally it will be subject to second-guessing (i.e., the business judgment rule will not necessarily apply). The more the board equips itself with information and analysis, the more likely its decisions will be sound and will be upheld.

The Sale of an ESOP-Owned Company

A series of issues with which majority and 100% ESOP-owned companies struggle is how to deal with offers to purchase the company and how the board should approach the sale of the company. In this context, it is important to understand the role that participants in the ESOP have the right to play in such a sale. I will first briefly review those rules and then outline my ideas about how the board should handle these questions.

ERISA Requirements

Under Section 409(e)(3) of the Code, participants must be given the right to direct the trustee of the ESOP to vote non-registered shares allocated to their accounts on all corporate matters involving "the voting of such shares with respect to the approval or disapproval of any corporate merger or consolidation, recapitalization, reclassification, liquidation, dissolution, sale of substantially all assets of a trade or business, or such similar transactions" as the Secretary of the Treasury may list in regulations. In addition to this legal proscription, most ESOP documents direct the ESOP trustee to vote unallocated shares in the same proportion that ESOP participants direct allocated shares in their accounts.

A few important caveats must be made at the outset. First, an ESOP trustee may be required to disregard the directions participants make regarding their allocated shares. The Department of Labor has written that the ESOP trustee should follow the participant's direction unless it can articulate well-founded reasons why the participant vote should be disregarded.[49] Further, in *Herman v. NationsBank Trust Company,*[50] the court determined that the trustee could not blindly follow the participants' directions regarding the unallocated shares. Instead, the ESOP trustee had to make an independent fiduciary decision.

---

49. DOL/PWBA letter, September 28, 1995, cited in Brown and Kober, "Legal, Tax, ERISA and Securities Issues," ¶13.3[4][c], n. 108, in Robert W. Smiley, Jr., et al., eds., *Employee Stock Ownership Plans* (Washington, D.C.: Beyster Institute, 2007), vol. 1.

50. 126 F.3d 1354 (11th Cir. 1997).

Dealing with Unsolicited Offers

A little bit later in this chapter, I will propose some relatively elaborate ideas for ESOP companies to consider inserting in their articles of incorporation and bylaws for dealing with unsolicited offers to purchase the company. In this section, I will offer some general observations about how the board should consider unsolicited offers.

Successful companies receive unsolicited offers to sell on a regular basis. Many of these offers are fishing expeditions designed simply for investment bankers or others to learn more about the company; some, though, are legitimate. In general, a board or a committee of the board has an obligation to consider bona fide offers to purchase the company. This is because the board's duty of care encompasses the need to derive the highest value for shareholders.

A company can adopt a "not for sale" policy that states it is not for sale generally except to fully funded offers that offer a significant premium in excess of current value. For example, one professional trustee has suggested to me that it would not recommend any sale that does not exceed the projected value of the company five years from the present. In addition, boards of directors may view the value of the company differently than the trustee's valuation advisor views the value of the company. For example, in a 100% ESOP owned S corporation, the board's financial advisors may legitimately place a higher premium on the value accruing to the fact the corporation does not pay taxes.

In any event, a board should develop a list of policies and procedures about how it will deal with unsolicited offers before offers are received. In addition, the board should appoint a committee that will review offers it deems bona fide on behalf of the board. What kinds of offers are bona fide? There can be no black-and-white answers. The committee will need to determine that in its best judgment. Many companies, of course, do not want to sell to outsiders, and that may have been a prime driver behind the decision to go ESOP. I will have some suggestions for such companies in the section below titled "Creative Drafting of Policies, Articles, and Bylaws for Companies that Want to Remain ESOP-Owned."

If the board believes that an offer is bona fide and that further negotiation is necessary, I believe it should enlist the services of an independent trustee as soon as possible so that it may take part in the negotiations. If the company is using an internal trustee, the potential conflicts of interest for the trustee will be too great. Also, the board committee negotiating the transaction along with management should also include outside members of the board.

Unless the transaction is a tender offer for shares, the board will need to vote on the transaction. This decision is a fiduciary decision, and the board must take care that it has had ample opportunity to review the offer from all perspectives. I believe that the board should engage its own financial advisor, and I further believe that the financial advisor should not have a stake in whether the transaction goes through or not. Even though the trust and participants will vote on the transaction, the board's fiduciary role is not diminished. If it recommends a transaction that a court later determines was a wrong decision, it can be held liable.

If the transaction is a tender offer for shares, then the trustee alone will make the decision about whether to engage in the transaction, and participants are not entitled to vote on the transaction under Code Section 409. For companies that wish to ensure that participants will always have the right to vote on whether to sell, there may be ways of amending corporate governance documents to ensure that this happens. I discuss this below.

Deciding to Sell When There Are No Offers

A company may reach a point where its directors determine that a sale of the company may be in the best interests of the company. This can happen for any number of reasons, but the most predominant is that the board decides that the company can no longer prosper as a standalone enterprise and that the value it currently has is as good as it is going to get. Hence, the board determines it will be best to sell out at or near the top of the market.

In this situation, the board will most likely engage the services of an investment bank or similar firm to solicit interest in the sale of the company. Once the board embarks on this path, it is possible that its only duty becomes to sell the company at the highest price. Accordingly, the board's decision to engage an investment banker should be carefully worded. For example, the board engagement of the investment banker should be couched initially as requesting that the banker investigate the market to determine how outside buyers might value the company in a proposed sale and what the terms of such a sale might be. Further, the board may want to set forth principles initially about the attributes it feels a successful suitor would have, such as a fully funded offer, a plan to grow the assets, and a commitment to maintain the business at its current sites for some period of time.

If the board is seriously embarking on a sale or auction, prudence would seem to dictate that in all but either the most preliminary of inquiries or the most distressed cases it should engage an independent trustee and keep the trustee informed of the process. In any event, the trustee will have to vote on the transaction and to pass on its fairness. Thus, keeping the trustee in the loop from the beginning will make the process smoother.

Creative Drafting of Policies, Articles, and Bylaws for Companies That Want to Remain ESOP-Owned

This section presents a series of practical concepts and steps that boards can take for written policies, the articles of incorporation, and bylaws to create a more highly functioning board and, if desired, to set forth a clear preference for the company to maintain its ESOP-owned structure. In this context, boards and shareholders may need to consider a number of amendments to the articles of incorporation and bylaws in connection with a minority or majority ESOP purchase.

One of the first steps a board of directors should undertake when considering any kind of ESOP transaction is to perform a careful review of the company's articles of incorporation and bylaws.[51] In this review the board should ask: Are there any provisions in the articles or bylaws that are inconsistent with the ESOP's ownership? Are there any provisions that could be added to make the operations of the company more efficient, such as creating board committees, allowing for meetings

51. The well-advised ESOP trustee will also perform this review as part of the purchase process and may ask for amendments to protect the interests of ESOP participants or simply to modernize the bylaws.

by teleconference, or allowing for resolution by written consent? Are the officers of the company accurately named and described? Has the company agreed to indemnify directors to the fullest extent provided by law? If not, should it?

As the board reviews the articles of incorporation and bylaws, there are a number of concepts the board absolutely should consider in the context of the ESOP becoming a shareholder. The list that follows is intended as a guide.

Amend the Articles to Provide That a Purpose of the Company Is to Be ESOP-Owned or Employee-Owned

One of the most challenging decisions that faces the board of an ESOP-owned company regardless of whether the ESOP is a minority shareholder or majority shareholder is whether to sell the company and what to do when unsolicited offers appear. One provision that could aid boards in the consideration of such problems is an amendment to the articles of incorporation that provides that in addition to the corporation having the purpose of conducting general legal business, it also has a purpose of becoming or being employee-owned, or even perhaps, ESOP-owned. This could be further refined by providing that the directors are entitled to reject offers for the company in acknowledgement of this provision in the articles.

Note, however, that this provision does not bind the ESOP trustee, nor would it necessarily release the board from all liability for not considering an outside bid. If a buyer were to make a direct solicitation to purchase shares from the ESOP trustee, this provision in the articles of incorporation would be of no binding authority on the ESOP trustee. Indeed, under Code Section 409, the ESOP trustee would not have to pass through the decision of whether to accept the tender offer to individual participants.

For example, a provision might read something like the following:

> The Company is formed to engage in any lawful undertakings, provided, however, that the shareholders intend that the Company be majority-owned by its employees through an Employee Stock Ownership Plan (the "ESOP"), as such is defined under Internal Revenue Code Section 4975, or any succes-

sor provision thereto. In furtherance thereof, the Board of Directors of the Company shall adopt such policies to encourage and further the employee ownership of the Company and to discourage a takeover of the Company by any party that would result in the termination of the ESOP. The Board shall be fully indemnified in adopting such policies as long as the Board can show that it reasonably believed the policy adopted would promote the ESOP ownership of the Company, even though such policy may result in, among other things, the discouragement of outside suitors for the Company or a lower share price value for the Company. The Board may submit such policies to a vote of the shareholders of the Company whenever the Board believes it is in the best interests of the Company to do so, even if the corporate law of [State] does not require such submission. In any event, the Board may determine in its sole discretion to reject without consideration any offer to purchase the Company that would eliminate the majority control of the ESOP over the Company, unless the Board has been expressly authorized by a majority of the ESOP participants to consider such offers.

Amend the Articles to Require That There Be Some Number of "Outside" Directors

Articles of incorporation typically do not include provisions regarding who the directors will be. However, it might make sense for the articles to be amended to provide for a certain number of "outside" directors. An outside director is a person serving as director who is neither an employee of or consultant to the company nor who has any significant contractual relationship to the company other than as a board member. As discussed earlier, from a corporate governance perspective, outside board members add value to a corporation because of their unbiased insight into the operations of the corporation.[52]

If the ESOP Is a Minority Shareholder, Amend the Articles to Give It a Special Class of Stock That Ensures It Will Elect Members to the Board

Typically, a corporation will provide that directors are elected by a majority of the shares. If an ESOP is a minority shareholder, it will

52. Indeed, it is my experience that valuation firms will look favorably upon a company having outside board members. See also William G. Bowen, *The Board Book* (New York City: W.W. Norton, 2008), 144 –48.

not be able to vote in any directors. It may make sense to create in the articles of incorporation a series of shares whereby the ESOP is given a special class that enables it to appoint one or more directors to the board even though the ESOP is a minority shareholder. This, coupled with the earlier provision concerning having outside directors, may give the ESOP the opportunity to bring outside eyes to bear on the company's day-to-day operations.

Amend the Articles to Provide That the Board Shall Look to Long-Term Rather Than Short-Term Growth and Shall Consider the Needs of Multiple Constituencies

One of the most complex series of decisions a board has to make is the balance between long-term growth and short-term gain. If, indeed, an outlook in favor of long-term growth is better for all of the various constituencies of the company, including the ESOP, then perhaps it makes sense to codify this rule within the articles of incorporation. By codifying it within the articles of incorporation, the board is protected, at least to some degree, in making decisions that favor long-term growth over short-term gains. This kind of provision, coupled with a provision requiring that the company be employee-owned, gives the board clear direction concerning how to handle such items as a sale of the business. This should create for the board a sort of cocoon that protects it from liability related to second-guessing if the board declines to review an offer to buy the company.

Amend the Bylaws to Create Board Committees with Oversight of Finance and Auditing, Employee and Board Development, and ESOP Relations

Most close corporations have very boilerplate bylaws that do not really consider a possibility of having shareholders who are not truly active in the business. One way of enhancing these bylaws would be to create under the bylaws a series of committees to govern different aspects of the board's work. It is particularly useful to have a finance/audit committee and a compensation committee. Moreover, in ESOP companies where continuing the ESOP culture is important, some sort of committee devoted to board succession planning, particularly creating a board that will continually be renewed in the understanding of the ESOP, can be a very helpful exercise. It will not be productive to the company if new board members are brought on who neither appreciate nor accept the ESOP structure.

Amend Articles and Bylaws to Permit Shareholder Action by Written Consent and/or to Permit Participant Voting for the Board Of Directors

The question of "circularity" is one of the more intriguing and sometimes troubling issues for companies that are majority or completely owned by an ESOP. This issue arises because under ERISA, the board of directors appoints the ESOP trustee, and, absent any special bylaw change, the ESOP trustee elects the board of directors. Thus, there is a circularity of appointment that is not broken by any legal device.

One way of dealing with this potential problem would be to adopt a bylaw or articles change to allow for shareholders to act by written consent. If an ESOP owns 100% of the company, its trustees could potentially toss out the board by written consent without ever calling a special meeting to do so. A second way of dealing with this issue would be to allow for participants in the ESOP to vote their shares in the election for the board of directors. Note that the board would still be responsible for putting up nominees, though conceivably the participants could conduct a proxy-style write-in campaign to elect their own nominees.

Consider a CTS-Style Voting Provision

In *CTS Corp. v. Dynamics Corp. of America,* the U.S. Supreme Court approved a state statute that allowed for a shareholder vote to allow the purchasing shareholder to vote its shares. The purpose of this kind of statute was to place tender offers on a playing field that was substantially similar to merger transactions (which require board and shareholder approval). ESOP companies may wish to adopt similar provisions in their articles (if permitted by state law) in order to place tender offers on a level playing field with merger and other Section 409 acquisitions.

Concluding Thoughts: Can We Construct a Perfect Governance Model for an ESOP Company?

It is clear that that the corporate laws that govern the lives of ESOP companies and their boards of directors are derived from a corporate and economic history that has little to do with the notion of shared or common capitalism. Still, it is not possible, or even desirable, to claim exemption from these rules unless such exemption were fundamental to the operation of the ESOP itself.[53] The principles in these laws, however, create not maximum standards but minimum requirements. These standards were not derived with the essence of common capitalism in mind. Moreover, these are the standards to which boards must adhere in order to *avoid* liability, not to advance the principles of a true ownership society.

Is it possible to create the ideal board structure that reinforces the employee incentive attributes of the ESOP? What might that look like? What might be the perfect ESOP company structure, and how would employees be involved in governance? How might a "perfect ESOP company" be constructed over time, and what would be the board's role? I offer the following as food for thought.

The perfect ESOP company structure will include multiple opportunities for feedback loops among the board, management, and employees. The ESOP structure requires an annual valuation, and, for the most part, this valuation is based on measurable company performance that can be tracked throughout the year. In addition, the valuation is based on projections against which the company's performance can be measured. So, in the perfect ESOP company structure, the company's performance would be explained and discussed among management and the board (i.e., the finance committee) and among management and the employees (through ESOP communication committees) on a regular basis. The goal of the communication would be to ensure that board, management, and employees all have expectations about the company that will be measured, reviewed, and adjusted over time.

53. Thus, if corporate law principles conflict with ERISA benefit principles, then the ERISA rule should preempt the corporate principle.

The expectation will not be for some happy workers' paradise but for concrete financial performance.

The perfect ESOP company structure will include the opportunity for employees to give feedback to management. Because many employees may not be able to become financially sophisticated, their feedback will come through financially sophisticated board members who are seen to represent the interests of employees. These board members will report directly to the employee/participants about the company.

The perfect ESOP company structure gives managers freedom to experiment so that they are not measured by how much they fail or succeed but by how hard they try. Independent board members will push insiders to grow the business at a reasonable level and to challenge themselves by approaching new opportunities.

In the perfect ESOP company, employees, management, and directors all will learn about what makes the company function best and what skills are needed at all levels. Employees will recognize that they have a duty to the company, just as the directors have duties to the shareholders and officers have duties to the directors. Through the financial discipline imposed by the transparent ESOP transaction, employees, management, and directors will achieve a rough consensus over time about what the right characteristics for the board are, and employees will ultimately be given the right to vote for the directors of the corporation. After all, if we trust them to vote for their president, for their congressional representatives, for their school boards and city councils, why shouldn't we entrust them with the vote for their board of directors?

(Appendix begins on next page)

APPENDIX

Many ESOP companies want to remain independent and ESOP-owned for as long as possible, yet they are unsure how to accomplish this task. What follows below are a series of suggested written policies, amendments to articles of incorporation, and bylaws that are intended as starting points for discussion with counsel.

1. Adoption of Policy Statement Regarding Employee Ownership

The board of directors would adopt the following policy statement:

> It is a goal of ________________ (the "Company") (i) to remain employee-owned through an Employee Stock Ownership Plan (the "ESOP") for as long as ownership by the ESOP is feasible; and (ii) to create a pattern of sustainable, prudently managed growth of the Company's revenues, profits and stock value all of which will, in turn, lead to a manageable repurchase obligation of shares of stock from participants in the ESOP as the Company grows.

2. Changes to the Articles of Incorporation

In support of the foregoing policy, the company's board of directors would recommend that the following language be added to the company's articles of incorporation:

> The Company is formed to engage in any lawful undertakings; *provided*, however, that the Company's shareholders have expressed a desire for the Company to be majority-owned by its employees through an Employee Stock Ownership Plan (the "ESOP") within the meaning of Section 4975 of the Internal Revenue Code. In furtherance thereof, the Board of Directors of the Company (the "Board") shall adopt and maintain policies to encourage and promote such employee ownership of the Company and to discourage any transaction that, upon completion, would result in a third party, and not the ESOP, being in control of the Company. The members of the Board shall be fully indemnified in adopting and maintaining such policies so long as such policies are reasonably believed to promote the ESOP ownership of the Company. This is so even though such policy(ies) may result in, among other things, the discouragement of outside suitors from making acquisition proposals to the Company. Such policies might also lead to lower valuations of the share prices for the Company's stock.

On a continuing basis, the Board may, but shall not be required to, submit such policies to a vote of the participants in the ESOP whenever the Board believes that it is in the best interests of the Company to do so. In any event, the Board may determine, in its sole discretion, to reject without negotiation any unsolicited acquisition proposal received by the Company if it would be likely to eliminate control of the Company by the ESOP, unless the ESOP participants first vote upon a resolution to explore such a transaction, which vote of participants shall be taken in the manner established from time to time by the Board of Directors, or as set forth in the Company's bylaws.

3. Changes to Bylaws

In support of the foregoing language in the articles of incorporation, the board would recommend the following additions to the company's bylaws:

Article ___

Provisions Relating to ESOP Control

Section 1. *General.* It is a goal of ___________________ (the "Company") to remain employee-owned through an Employee Stock Ownership Plan (the "ESOP") for so long as such ownership structure is feasible.

Section 2. *Periodic Solicitation of ESOP Participants' Views.* At a special meeting to be called by the Board of Directors, at the time and place of its choosing, the views of ESOP participants shall be solicited and heard on the issue of whether the Board of Directors should reconsider the Company's policy of remaining independent and controlled by the ESOP. The Board of Directors shall then reconsider such independence and ESOP control policy only if there is a Supermajority Participant Vote which, for purposes of this Article ___, is a vote by at least seventy-five percent (75%) of the ESOP participants and the beneficial holders of seventy-five percent (75%) of the stock held by the ESOP in favor of a resolution to reconsider such policy (with ESOP shares held in suspense deemed voted in the same proportion as shares allocated to participants' accounts).

Section 3. *Other Circumstances.* Among the factors that (i) the Board of Directors shall consider in calling a meeting to solicit ESOP participants' views, and (ii) the ESOP participants shall consider in voting on a resolution to reconsider the Company's policy of remaining independent and controlled by the ESOP are: (a) whether the long-term viability of the Company is challenged by unfavorable market conditions, (b) whether technological changes jeopardize the Company's survival as an independent entity, or (c) whether employees and the Board of Directors have lost confidence in the management leadership of the Company. The decision to solicit third party acquisition proposals under this Section 3 shall be made only after approval by the Board of Directors followed by a Supermajority Participant Vote and approval of the ESOP trustee.

Section 4. *Preference for ESOP Suitors.* If the Board of Directors determines to solicit third party acquisition proposals, the Board may give preference to buyers that have employee ownership or that will maintain the ESOP.

Section 5. *Other General Provisions.* The Board of Directors shall ensure that any transaction involving the sale of all or substantially all of the Company's assets or capital stock which the Board of Directors resolves to pursue must be conditioned as to completion upon receiving a Supermajority Participant Vote in favor of same.

Section 6. *Repeal or Amendment of This Article.* This Article may only be repealed or amended if such repeal or amendment is approved by (a) at least two-thirds of members of the Board of Directors and (b) Supermajority Participant Vote.

CHAPTER 2

Serving on an ESOP Company Board: Reflections of ESOP Board Members

Corey Rosen

What is it like to serve as an outside board member in an ESOP company? While the rest of this book explores the legal, financial, and business issues board members must understand, this chapter looks at what several outside board members told me about their experiences on ESOP company boards.

To make it possible for those interviewed to be candid in their comments, I have provided only minimal information about the companies involved. Where there are potentially more confidential issues involved, I have not attributed comments to the person on that board, but simply to "one of the interviewees."

I interviewed seven outside board members:

- Bill Allaire has worked for years in the technology sector, but also has started his own company and has served on the board of a number of nonprofits. He has had a particular interest in special needs children. He serves on the board of a large, 100% ESOP-owned company providing client services.
- Lee Bloom is the owner and managing director of Aldine Advisors, a professional services firm providing financial decision support to privately held and small-cap publicly traded companies. He was previously with the investment banking firm Duff & Phelps, where he acquired considerable experience with ESOPs. He serves on four ESOP company boards, including one unionized services company with several hundred employees, a smaller unionized manufacturing company, and two other services companies, one that is very large and one that is mid-sized. All are 100% ESOP-owned.

- Ronald Ludwig was widely considered the leading legal expert on ESOPs during his years in private practice. He was very active in the NCEO and the ESOP Association. He is now retired from his law practice and serves on the boards of four companies, three of which are 100% ESOP-owned and the fourth of which formerly had an ESOP.
- Lee Morgan is the retired president of a large 100% ESOP-owned company that had been in his family for three generations before becoming employee-owned. He still serves on that board. He also serves on the board of a mid-sized technical services company that is 33% ESOP-owned, which was the focus of his interview for this chapter.
- Randy Rowland is the president of the consulting firm Teams*work* LLC, which provides assistance to ESOP and non-ESOP companies in creating and sustaining high-involvement management systems. He created a 100% ESOP at the insurance company Bertholon-Rowland in 1990. He now serves on the board of a mid-sized manufacturing company 100% owned by its ESOP.
- Robert Sanchez is the CFO of National Wire and Cable Company, an ESOP- owned company, and serves on its board. For purposes of this chapter, however, I interviewed him for his service on a 100% ESOP-owned mid-sized financial services company.
- Teri Wolfe is the former vice president for human resources at Patagonia. She later started her own organizational development firm, which currently works with mission-driven organizations. She now serves on the board of a 100% ESOP-owned company in the food business.

Among them, these seven interviewees serve on the boards of 14 ESOP companies.

Characteristics of the Boards

The boards typically vary in size from five to nine members. Two interviewees also served on boards in their own companies, one of which has no outsiders and one of which has a minority of outsiders.

This chapter, however, focuses on their experiences outside their own companies. All of these have at least one outsider, and about two-thirds have a majority of insiders. Three of the companies have one or more non-management employees on the board. We did not poll how many boards have an internal trustee on the board (none had an external trustee), but two of the interviewees mentioned that they do have this arrangement. Board meetings are typically held every quarter, with additional committee meetings one or more times per year.

Thirteen of the 14 boards have committees. Those with committees each have an audit committee and a committee overseeing executive compensation (in some cases this is a compensation committee, and in other cases a personnel committee oversees compensation for executives as well as broader personnel issues). Most companies have a governance committee that, among other things, selects new board nominees and reviews and revises corporate bylaws. Less frequent committees are operations, pensions, acquisitions, and investments.

ESOP Legal Issues and the Board

ESOP company board members face an added complexity compared to boards in non-ESOP companies because they must at least be somewhat conversant in ESOP law and practice. Ronald Ludwig, however, noted that the "primary ERISA duty for the board is to decide who will manage the ESOP. Boards need to exercise considerable care both in selecting and monitoring the ESOP fiduciary. But dealing with ESOP issues is not the most significant element of board responsibility." Bill Allaire agreed. "In many ways, ESOP boards are very much the same as non-ESOP boards, but the relationship between trustee and board can be a challenge, and all the rules are complicated. Still, dealing with ESOP issues is not the most significant side of the responsibility." Randy Rowland, who had served on the board before the company became an ESOP, had a somewhat different perspective. "Once we became a 100% ESOP," he said, "nothing changed and everything changed. Laws didn't really change, but there is now a new awareness of the ESOP constituency as well as the intricacies of ESOP law. But not every director puts that at the front of their mind; to some, the ESOP was primarily a financing tool, not a core change in corporate operations."

Formal training on ESOP issues also varies. Teri Wolfe said at her company "all board members go to one annual ESOP meeting per year. Soon after, the board meets to assess what they heard and learned and to discuss how to use this information." Bill Allaire said there was "no special training at first, but now there are some written materials, online resources, and experts brought in to make presentations." Ronald Ludwig said the experience varies at the boards he is on. "In one case, board members schedule a session with an outside party to provide education. In the others, there is no formal training, but there is informal training based on the needs and desires of board members. On one board, the ESOP committee elects the board based on a list of criteria, one of which is knowledge of ESOPs." Lee Bloom said that at three of the four boards he serves on there has been informal training from outsiders when needed, although a number of the board members already were conversant with ESOP issues.

The interviewees vary in how important they think the issue of training is. In a number of cases, at least some board members were selected because of their ESOP knowledge or had it as a function of their position with the company. Ronald Ludwig said it was not necessary for everyone to be familiar with ESOP issues, but Lee Bloom noted that a lack of training can cause problems. "Decisions can get made with respect to executive pay, repurchase obligation, and ESOP contribution levels when board members don't know much about the issues. Also, when looking at acquisition issues, there is more of a need to understand the economics of an ESOP company." Two of the interviewees also said they believed it was important for board members to understand how ESOP companies can and should be different in terms of organizational culture.

Interaction with the Trustee and Employees

ESOP boards are widely divergent in how they deal with trustees and employees. Common trustee practices include:

- Having trustees on the board. Usually these are insiders, such as a CFO, but some outside trustees are on boards as well. (Outside trustees differ on this issue, but most take the position that it is better not to serve on the board in order not to compromise their independence.)

- Having trustees observe board meetings and answer questions but not vote on issues.
- Having trustees formally report to the board on a regular basis.
- Having only a written report to the board from trustees.

Interactions with employees are similarly diverse:

- Having one or more nonmanagement employees elected to the board or having representation from an ESOP committee on the board.
- Having an employee advisory committee to meet with the board, but without formal board membership.
- Allowing employees to observe board meetings, usually by inviting one or more to specific meetings. In a few cases, larger groups of employees may observe board meetings held in a suitable venue.
- Sending minutes or summaries of board meetings to employees.
- Having no formal interactions.

Our interviewees had similar experiences. Ronald Ludwig said that at one company where he is a director, there is overlap between the ESOP committee and the board; in another, the ESOP counsel prepares a report on the board meetings to share with employees; in still another, the ESOP committee makes a full annual report. Lee Bloom said that the trustee of one company meets with the board; in the other companies, the ESOP fiduciary committee and board overlap. Bloom said this overlap could raise an issue because each group may have different fiduciary concerns. Teri Wolfe and Bill Allaire said that board membership and trustees overlap, but neither reported any problems coming out of this. Randy Rowland reported that the trustee meets with the board regularly to provide reports.

Bill Allaire and Lee Morgan said in their companies there is a formal system for interacting with or reporting to employees. Bill Allaire said reports from the board are provided to managers, who can then report the information to employees. The process provides a mechanism for feedback to the board, but he said it has not been used much. Lee Morgan said employees vote for board members, and there are informal reports from board meetings. The geographical spread of the company, however, makes the process more challenging. In the company where he was the CEO, he added, an employee committee elects the board and serves as a liaison to the broader work force.

Acquisition Offers

Offers to buy a company often present the most serious challenge a board faces. Depending on state laws and corporate bylaws or charters, boards can have varying latitude in how they react to offers. While all boards can ignore offers not considered to be serious (such as letters from brokers looking for companies for sale, letters sent to multiple companies, offers that do not show evidence of financial or management capability, and so on), they do have to look at legitimate offers. If allowed, the board may consider issues other than purely financial benefits to owners, such as maintaining employment, remaining employee-owned, pursuing a corporate mission, or other specific concerns.

The ESOP trustee, however, has a more narrowly defined obligation to support offers that are in the long-term financial interest of plan participants as shareholders, not as employees. That does not mean that any offer at a premium should be accepted. The trustee might conclude participants are better off with the company staying independent because there is greater potential future value due to a combination of increasing share price and higher contribution rates. A trustee might also agree that an offer is at a premium, but a better offer could be had down the road.

Nonetheless, there is potential for conflict, at least in theory, even if unwanted takeovers are extremely rare. A board, for instance, might ignore or reject an offer because of concerns about what the buyer would do with the business, but the trustee might want the offer to be considered. In that case, the trustee could pressure the board and even threaten to sue if the board does not act.

Some of the interviewees reported that they only had received, in Robert Sanchez's terms, "fishing expeditions." He believes that the

ESOP, and the board's desire to stay independent, would deter any potential investors, who would simply move on to easier targets. Bill Allaire said that while financial issues would have to be the paramount concern, some of the players who could make offers one day were "bad actors" the company would not want to be acquired by. Lee Bloom said that the companies where he is on the board have also not yet had to respond to a serious offer, but, if they did, financial concerns would be the most important factor. Randy Rowland said that if there were a serious offer, the fact that the company has an independent, outside trustee would be very helpful. While the board and trustee would not be eager to sell, he said a significant premium—"north of 20%"—would need to be considered carefully.

Ronald Ludwig said the companies where he serves have a commitment to remain employee-owned. One company did have a serious offer but decided not to sell. He said that the board's responsibility is tricky in an ESOP company. "From a corporate law standpoint," he said, "maintaining employee ownership can be a legitimate concern for boards. But ERISA makes the issue more financial for trustees. In practice, the result is almost always that unwanted offers do not go anywhere, but there is a potential for conflict."

Teri Wolfe's company has had many conversations on the subject of acquisitions. "We always want to be ready for the possibility. There are some intrinsic conflicts between weighing interests of shareholders and employees. The board has stated that they want to have a policy of sustainability as a philosophical basis for the corporate charter. They consider employee ownership from a holistic standpoint and have actually registered as a 'B' corporation, a non-legally binding corporate form that commits the company to look beyond just investment return to community, the quality of employment, the environment, and other broader issues."

In one situation, however, the sale of one of the companies on whose board a respondent serves became a real possibility. In this case, the board took the initiative to look for a buyer as a way to deal with a financial crisis the company was facing. As it turned out, an acceptable buyer was not found, and the economic situation has turned around sufficiently that this course of action may not be needed.

Executive Pay

The interviewees all agreed that overseeing executive pay is an essential board function that deserves careful attention. Most would agree with Randy Rowland that in setting executive pay, "it's not like going from capitalism to socialism. The challenge is getting the best people to come to work there when those people can get equity elsewhere. In 100% ESOP companies, all they can get is synthetic equity." But he said that synthetic equity has worked acceptably "as long as cash flow is there and the 409(p) rules are met." (Section 409(p) rules are designed to prevent excessive real or synthetic equity benefits in an S corporation with an ESOP from going to too few people.)

Lee Bloom said greedy management had not been a problem, but, he said, "coming up with the right mix of incentives is a challenge. For instance, if the primary metric is growth in EBITDA, executives might focus on earnings. But that may not be the best way to measure management performance, especially over the short term. For instance, management could try to grow EBITDA through acquisitions, even if there might be other, better uses for the money. Moreover, if the acquisition brings positive EBITDA, you [the executive] just bought it, rather than grew it."

Lee Morgan and Bob Sanchez said their companies looked primarily at market-driven comparisons. Sanchez said that this had been challenging, with the board still trying to find the right balance between providing enough incentives for key people without being excessive. Teri Wolfe said her company took a somewhat different approach. "We want to make sure that relative compensation for all employees is reasonable." (This concept of "internal equity" is gaining some favor in public companies.)

Other Major Challenges

All of the directors said that it is very important to have people on the board who are independent of management and agreed that it is more difficult when the board is made up entirely or primarily of insiders. "The critical issue is having people who can challenge the CEO in a way insiders just cannot do," Bob Sanchez said. "No matter what their relationship with their boss, insiders (other than the CEO) are going to naturally think twice about challenging a CEO on a board." Attracting qualified and motivated outside directors, therefore, is an ongoing necessity.

Randy Rowland and Bob Sanchez both said that the board needs to help nurture the distinctive culture that makes employee ownership successful. That can be difficult when board members are selected for their industry expertise and contacts but may not have experience with employee ownership or a philosophical inclination toward the kind of high-involvement cultures that make employee ownership work best.

Bill Allaire added that the repurchase obligation is a major concern. While the company is currently able to handle that liability, boards need to be vigilant in monitoring the issue.

Two companies dealt with regulatory issues, in one case resulting in a change in board composition. In both instances, the regulatory problems were successfully addressed, with the board providing input into the process.

Conclusion

As outside directors, it is not surprising that the people we interviewed believed that having outside directors was highly advisable. As Ronald Ludwig put it, "ESOP companies are moving more towards a public company model." While full-blown compliance with Sarbanes-Oxley (which applies only to public companies) or best practices recommended by shareholder groups would be beyond the capacity of most closely held companies, many of the principles can be adapted to the ESOP company context, such as independent compensation committees.

Many of the respondents noted that the outside directors bring valuable business insights and contacts, while those familiar with ownership culture issues help keep this essential aspect of ESOPs front and center.

As ESOPs mature, there seems to be little doubt that outside directors will become more prevalent. This chapter presents the views of just several of these directors, but companies should be able to find other companies in their area or industries with outside directors to seek their input as well.

CHAPTER 3

The Role of the Board in ESOP Companies

Cecil Ursprung

When society consisted mainly of hunters and gatherers, were there boards of directors? How about during the agricultural era? Or the Middle Ages, when craftspeople and guilds emerged? Or the merchant era, when countries such as England, France, and Spain were building empires?

Boards arguably go back to medieval times, when societies of independent merchants created boards to govern their joint activities. The concept of boards migrated to some of the early large businesses, as evidenced by board statutes in 1694 for the Bank of England. Colonial and trading companies chartered by the king were required to have boards, a practice that may have influenced the development of boards in the U.S.

But the board as a ubiquitous institution really only emerged in the 19th century. Before that time, most "work organizations" consisted of single individuals who owned and managed their own economic entities. If the same person owns, manages, and produces work output, there is no purpose for a board. Even with the rise of the merchant class and trading activities that extended throughout the world, there was often no need for the oversight function of the board because each voyage was organized by a venturer, and the arrangement was terminated and profits distributed when the voyage was complete.

By the 19th century, as businesses became larger, more complex, and more permanent, ownership and management were more likely to be separate individuals or institutions, and ownership felt a growing need to oversee management. That was especially true when ownership and management were geographically distant. Owner-managed firms often sought boards as well, however, as sources of advice. In the U.S., corporate law has required boards of directors since 1811, when New York passed a law that soon was imitated by other states.

The Role of a Board

There are two factors that heavily influence the role of a board in any privately held company. Those are the status of ownership and the status of leadership within the organization. In general, the broader the ownership of the company in terms of number of owners, and the further from the first generation of leadership the company has traveled, the larger the probability that the board will be heavily populated by independent directors and actively involved in the affairs of the company on a strategic level.

These two factors—ownership and leadership status—often play a key role when owner-founder firms transition to organizations owned by employees and led by professional managers. In founder-owned companies, boards are often passive and populated by family and close associates. Another frequent option chosen by founder-owners is the advisory board, which has no legal status and authority but may have considerable influence on the leader. As ownership becomes less concentrated and the founder transitions out of leadership, boards may over time become more active and independent. This tendency toward more active independent boards also is evident if owner-founder managed firms become publicly owned or are sold to investment groups.

Jack Veale, a consultant to privately held companies, has identified five types of board practice:

1. *The passive board:* The passive board may have few or no independent directors, and if they are present, they are probably trusted lawyers, accountants, or bankers who may not pass the common definition of "independent," due to their supplier relationship with the company. This board will probably have a strong founding CEO who serves both the roles of CEO and chairman. The CEO calls the meetings of the board whenever he or she deems it necessary and controls the function and actions of the board. There is limited activity and participation by board members and limited accountability. The purpose of the board is principally to ratify management decisions and make them legal.
2. *The certifying board:* The certifying board is somewhat more active than the passive board. Its principal function is to certify to the

shareholders that the CEO is performing according to expectations. This board has a great need for independent directors who are willing to change management if needed to be credible to the owners. In these boards, the CEO is likely to be evaluated by the external board members.

3. *The engaged board:* This board is easily more active than the previous two. It is heavily populated with outsiders who provide inside advice and support to the CEO and the management team. There is a high level of interaction and discussion at board meetings. The engaged board takes time to define the roles and responsibilities of board members and the boundaries and responsibilities of both the board and the CEO. An engaged board is likely to have several committees, such as the audit committee, the compensation committee, and the governance committee. This board understands it is ultimately responsible for oversight of the CEO and company performance as well as succession planning. This board will sometimes seek outside experts that can add value to its decision-making process.
4. *The intervening board:* An intervening board is usually found in a crisis situation such as an absent or dysfunctional CEO. It is characterized by frequent meetings on short notice and intense involvement with key crisis issues. The primary focus is on achieving action plans to correct the current situation.
5. *The operating board*: The operating board is also heavily populated by independent directors and is often found in start-up environments such as new companies or new divisions with outside financing. This group may make key decisions as a group that management then implements. The population of the group helps fill in management experience gaps. The group tends to be hands-on, focusing on selected high-priority activities such as developing product market systems, staffing, or financing the organization.

According to the National Association of Corporate Directors, to be effective, any board must be made up of the right people who operate within a culture that emphasizes and promotes candid communication and rigorous decision-making. The group must set relevant strategic issues and focus on those that will help the company maximize its long-term value. In this environment, that board must be provided with the right information and have a robust process for making informed decisions and holding management accountable for results.

Within this context, the most important role of a board is to select the CEO and provide for leadership and development and succession processes for the CEO and the senior management team. In addition, there is legal foundation as well as historic precedent for the board performing an oversight function: Are promised results achieved? Are plans realized? Is the conduct of the company within established guidelines for agreed-upon ethics and principles? In addition to these questions, the board is often called upon to provide guidance to management decision-making. Here, the boundaries between board and CEO functions can sometimes be tested. However, the board does have a responsibility to transfer the experience of its members to those entrusted with making decisions on a contemporaneous basis. Increasingly, especially in companies with diverse ownership, the board is called on to oversee regulatory compliance. Historically, this meant working with the auditors on accurate financial statements, but more recently the role has been broadened to include compliance with government regulations, governance regulations, and legislation such as Sarbanes-Oxley. Finally, with increasing frequency, the board has played an active role in communications with shareholders. These communications may take place routinely at annual meetings and in quarterly reports, but they may also occur on special occasions such as CEO succession or major news events.

Over the past decade, boards have, by necessity, become much more activist, especially in companies where management and ownership are substantially separated. For example:

- There is a clear trend toward an increasing number of "independent" directors and a decreasing number of "insiders."
- As the incidence of management lapses, abuses, and fraud has increased, board committees have become more active and independent, and oversight has increased.
- In response to shareholder pressure, boards have become increasingly intolerant of poor performance by those who lead.

While these trends, and governmental effort to correct abuse through regulation, have been aimed primarily at public companies, the impact has often been clearly felt in the private company sector. As shareholder activism increases, board oversight will continue to increase in response.

Board Makeup

The appropriate makeup of the board is heavily dependent on which stages the board is in. For example, passive boards may be populated by a limited number of family members and trusted advisors who have economic relationships with the company. This may work fine in a situation where a strong CEO controls the board function and the ownership of the company. But as companies grow more diverse in their ownership and as management moves beyond the first generation, a strong case can be made for increasing the population of truly independent outside board members. Companies in such situations should give careful thought to the skills and experience needed on the board. Examples of high-priority skills include prior or present CEOs, considerable financial expertise outside the United States, knowledge of the industry, and experience in the marketplace or with the technology owned by the company. As a group, directors should thoroughly understand the company's business, industry, and competition. The board should be a source for quality ideas, contacts, and support for best practices. Board members should understand the development and execution of appropriate company strategies, and they should be able to establish high (and measurable) standards for senior management performance. Board members should provide a key support role in attracting a top leadership team and creatively linking management compensation to the creation of shareholder value. Thus, a good board member will have a variety of skills and experiences to bring to the board and a depth of experience that may not be present anywhere in the existing organization.

Good members insist on timely and accurate information necessary to make quality decisions. They also insist on honesty and forthrightness on the part of management. Good board members are willing do their homework, study issues in advance, and participate actively in board discussions, including the constructive use of dissent where appropriate. A fully engaged board can be a powerful influence in the focus on and achievement of worthy company goals.

Recruitment, Orientation, and Compensation

With some exceptions, board members for most companies can be found within a one- to two-hour drive from headquarters or another frequent meeting place. Exceptions might be someone who is particularly well steeped in the company's technology or has an unusual degree of industry knowledge. If the recruitment focus is local, it is probably best to shy away from social clubs and nonprofits in favor of referrals from existing board members; recommendations from local lawyers, accountants and bankers; and members of certain relevant organizations, such as a business and industry association, the National Association of Corporate Directors, or a member of the local World Affairs Council. Before any recruitment efforts, there should be a job description or profile written for each set of experiences desired on the board. Examples might include one for CEO experience, one for financial expertise, one for knowledge of the business processes (science, manufacturing technology, marketing strategies, and so on) of the company, and one for international experience. Such people should be in the stage of their careers where they are ready and willing give something back and have the time to do so.

As a general rule, it is advisable to have three to five candidates for each board member slot. This implies an initial screening process. The initial screenings can be done by comparing resumes submitted to job profiles. Here, the idea is looking for matches between a candidate's experience and the requirements of the job. Once the initial screening takes place, usually by a member of the governance committee, a series of interviews can begin with members of the committee or the committee as a whole. Once the committee has a slate for consideration by the full board, there should be an opportunity for the candidates to present themselves to the full board and for one-on-one interaction and evaluation. It is only after these efforts, which may go on for several months, that the board feels confident and comfortable to recommend a slate to shareholders.

Once members have been approved by the shareholders, it is necessary for maximum board effectiveness to conduct a thorough multimonth orientation program, which should involve such things as the reading of a year or more of past board minutes, the study of company product brochures, a thorough review of the financial statements with the CFO of the company, tours of the facilities, and interviews with members of senior management. Too often, board members are asked to give thoughtful advice and make informed decisions in the absence of a high-quality orientation program. If a high-quality program is implemented, a "catch as catch can" three-year orientation process can be accomplished in three months with obvious benefit to the company, its shareholders, and senior management.

Compensation matters can be a thorny issue, especially in private companies. While board member compensation is a matter of public record in public companies, private companies have no obligation to disclose this information and often decline to do so. Two general rules seem to apply: the larger the company the higher the compensation, and the higher the risk (as in public companies) the higher the compensation. As a starting point, one might consider using data from the annual National Association of Corporate Directors compensation surveys for public companies, and the biannual survey of compensation and activity and governance activity in private companies. The compensation in public companies should probably be viewed as an upper boundary by private companies since some level of discount factor applies due to the increased risk of serving on a public company board.

The Evolution of the Board at Reflexite Corporation from 1970 to the Present

My company, Reflexite Corporation, was founded in1970 by two brothers and their brother-in-law. In the early days, the board consisted of the three owners, and they met only when necessary to fulfill legal requirements. However, things changed in 1977 when they sold 25% of Reflexite to a customer company and 10% to two employees. At that point, the board was expanded from three to eight members: the original three, two representatives from the customer company, the company's banker and lawyer, and a local business executive who was a good friend of the founding brothers. The result was that a 25% owner also had 25% of the board seats. This board met from two to four times per year. At the request of the founders and the company lawyer, the meetings were informal, as reflected in the brief meeting notes of that era.

In 1983, when the brothers were in their mid-60s, a successor president (myself) was hired from outside the company and elected to the board, and discussions about the future ownership of the company became a frequent topic at board meetings.

In 1985, the founders and I decided to transition significant ownership to an ESOP, and I requested support for building a stronger, more involved outside board of directors to provide appropriate guidance and oversight. With the first ESOP transaction, the number of owners expanded from 5 to 85, and the lawyer, banker, and friend were replaced by local businesspeople with no connection to the company other than their membership on the board. The Reflexite board evolved from a small group meeting minimum legal requirements to a fully functioning board with three committees and eight members as the company evolved from its birth in 1970 to $10 million in sales and 100 employee-owners in 1990. The evolution continued as the company reached its current size (as of 2009) of $80 million in sales and 450 employee-owners.

In 2006, one third of the company was sold by long-term investors to an outside institutional investment company. As a result, the board was expanded from eight to eleven members to achieve an equitable balance of membership interests. There is general agreement that the number should be reduced over time toward seven to eight. Members have diverse experience and expertise, as shown in table 3-1.

Table 3-1. Experience of Reflexite Board Members

Type of Experience	Number of Reflexite Board Members with Such Experience
CEO	4
CFO	3
Technology	2
Corporation finance/transactions	2
International business	6

Because some of the members have more than one area of expertise, the total exceeds eleven. Of the eleven members, two are insiders and nine are outsiders. The board meets four to six times per year.

There are four board committees:

1. *The executive committee.* Consists of the chairman and two other board members to act for the full board in emergencies. It has not met in the past decade because the board has a preference for full board meetings whenever possible.
2. *The compensation committee.* Responsible for determining the compensation for the board, the CEO, and his direct reports. Also responsible for broad-based equity compensation (ESOP, options, ESPP) and cash bonus systems. It meets four to six times per year.
3. *The audit and finance committee.* Responsible for the annual certified audit, ethics policies, capital structure, and financial projections. It meets three to five times per year.
4. *The governance committee.* Responsible for governance issues, such as committee structure, compliance with regulatory requirements, determination of management vs. board responsibilities, and nominations to the board. It meets two to three times per year.

In addition, there are three business unit advisory boards, which provide advice and counsel to the leadership of the company's three business units. There are composed of both outside board members and members of senior management. Meetings are held approximately twice per year.

In large measure, the high level of board activity results from three major changes taking place within the company: a change in business strategy, a CEO succession, and a change in ownership. There is an expectation that the level of activity will decline as these changes are successfully implemented.

Conclusion

The Reflexite board is more institutionalized and more developed than most boards in ESOP companies. While many ESOP companies are moving toward more formal board structures, informal boards, made up largely of insiders, remain the norm. In my experience, however, the investment of time and money in our board has been an excellent investment, helping the company prosper and maintaining a high level of credibility with our employee owners and outside owners.

CHAPTER 4

Directors, Officers, and Fiduciary Liability Insurance for ESOP Companies

John D. Schlichte
Michael Wade

On any given day, you can read articles in business publications on the mismanagement of various companies. The list is long, and such mismanagement affects the lives of thousands of employees, vendors, the community, and ultimately the consumers. Due to the lack of corporate governance for some companies, it is appropriate that we review the general duties of directors and officers ("D&O") before discussing directors and officers insurance ("D&O insurance").

Duties of Directors and Officers

A corporation's directors and officers must manage the company in the stockholders' best interest. This involves three primary duties for directors and officers. They are the duty of care or due diligence, the duty of loyalty, and the duty of obedience.

- The duty of care requires the director or officer to be familiar with the finances and activities of the organization. It also requires the director to act in "good faith" using the diligence, care, and skill of a prudent person in a similar situation. Some of the responsibilities of directors are to attend board meetings, review prior meeting minutes, establish the process of approval for major obligations, record votes for or against a company's directives, participate in risk assessment and strategic planning, and review indemnification of its officers and directors.

- The duty of loyalty requires the review of conflicts of interest, transactions involving board members and officers, and the code of ethics.
- The duty of obedience requires the director or officer to comply with all applicable laws and to act in accordance with the organization's resources and purpose.

Directors and officers of privately held companies operate in a business environment increasingly characterized by litigious behavior. Unlike publicly traded companies that are held to laws such as the Sarbanes-Oxley Act of 2002 that require, among other things, the rotation of auditors, corporate responsibility, and corporate fraud accountability, many privately held companies do not perceive a need to purchase D&O insurance. In fact, most privately held companies do not purchase D&O coverage. A prudent individual considering serving on a board of directors would be wise to review the company's current coverages that are in place to indemnify them.

In 2005, Chubb interviewed 451 U.S. executives from privately owned companies in 46 states to gain a better understanding of the exposures and insurance needs of privately held companies. The survey, which was gathered over a five-year period, provided the following information:

- Twenty-six percent of the companies experienced a D&O lawsuit in the past five years.
- Seventy-two percent of the companies that experienced a D&O lawsuit thought they would have another lawsuit in the coming year.
- Twenty-seven percent of the executives responding to the survey expected their companies to make an acquisition during the next 12 months.
- In a defensive measure against D&O lawsuits, 24% of the companies had adopted the governance and accountability provisions of the Sarbanes-Oxley Act of 2002, even though Sarbanes-Oxley governs only public companies.
- The average claim was $308,475.

- D&O lawsuits were generated by a few key common drivers:
  - Forty-three percent of lawsuits were customer-initiated.
  - Twenty-nine percent of lawsuits were initiated by a government agency.
  - Seventeen percent of lawsuits resulted from vendors.
  - Eleven percent of lawsuits were from partners or shareholders.[1]

Based on the responsibilities of a director and officer and the survey by Chubb, there appears to be a wide disparity between the perceived risk and the actual purchase of D&O insurance. The misconceptions could be based on the following:

- Executives may mistakenly believe their existing company insurance policy provides coverage for directors and officers.
- Financial operations for privately held companies are under less scrutiny than for public companies.
- Small companies generally do not have the same issues as large companies.
- The cost for the protection is too expensive.
- The insurance consultant did not raise this issue.
- There may be confusion about the need for insurance.

Legal Exposure for Directors and Officers

There are several sources of legal exposure for directors and officers:

- Claims by shareholders, particularly within an ESOP, may not be covered under the traditional D&O policy but may be covered under the fiduciary liability policy.

---

1. Employee lawsuits are covered by employment practices liability insurance and are not covered under D&O insurance due to the insured v. insured exclusion.

- Claims by customers or suppliers for breach of contract, trademark infringement, and disclosure of trade secrets may arise.
- Claims from government regulators can include claims for environmental issues, employee safety compliance, and other regulatory issues.
- Claims from creditors and lenders may be for inaccurate financial statements, including claims stemming from a lack of disclosure of financial information relevant to the operation of the business.
- Claims from competitors could include false advertising, misrepresentation, and deceptive trade practices.

It is evident from the information listed above that risk is present and that directors and officers should consider purchasing D&O insurance.

Components of D&O Insurance

When securing D&O coverage, caveat emptor. Unlike many traditional insurance policies, D&O insurance coverage is not standardized among insurance companies. Policies are generally divided into three classes of business: non-profit, private, and publicly traded. The type of ownership will dictate the policy type required. Generally, all policies will have a "claim made" date or a retroactive date, where the policy date will be the start date for coverage, excluding all prior acts. The typical policy structure is comprised of five major components, which are described below:

1. Insuring agreements
2. Definitions
3. Exclusions
4. Limits
5. General or other conditions

1. Insuring Agreements

Insuring agreements identify who is an insured under the policy. This may sound fairly straightforward, but identifying past, present, and future directors and officers and their impact on an organization can be a challenging task. There can also be various subsidiaries and other holding companies that were acquired, merged, or divested during the policy period. With this in mind, most D&O insurance policies are written under a single policy with three separate insuring agreements commonly referred to as agreements A, B, and C. Determining which coverage is needed and in what amount is a matter of careful planning, review of applicable state laws, and advice from trusted advisors such as CPAs, insurance consultants, and legal counsel.

- *D&O Liability (Side "A")*

  Side "A" will pay for a covered loss when the insured director or officer is not indemnified by the organization. Under side "A" coverage, the insured consists only of the directors and officers, not the organization. Lack of indemnification by the organization can stem from the following:

  — The corporation is not financially capable of indemnifying the director or officer.

  — In the event of a derivative lawsuit, directors and officers are required to pay settlement or judgment.

  — Bylaws or state statutes do not require the entity to indemnify directors and officers.

  Directors and officers belonging to subsidiaries acquired after the effective date of the policy may be covered by notifying the insurance company, subject to the terms and conditions of the policy. The policy also will cover claims made against the personal assets of the director or officer, including claims made against the director or officer's estate, heirs, and legal representatives arising out of their status as such.

- *Corporate Reimbursement (Side "B")*

  This coverage pays on behalf of the insured company named in the policy. It will pay for covered losses occurring during the policy period or within the retroactive date only if the directors and officers are entitled to indemnification by the company for damages, judgments, costs, and expenses as a result of the defense of any action, lawsuit, or proceeding. The company reimbursement coverage can also cover any subsidiary acquired after the policy inception date or within the period covered by the retroactive date. This particular coverage is important due to the indemnification statues in most states. Bylaws or articles of incorporation are set up to reimburse the directors or officers for expenses incurred while acting in their duty to the organization.

- *Entity Coverage (Side "C")*

  D&O insurance policies are designed to indemnify the individual director or officer or the organization when it incurs the cost to indemnify the director and officer for a wrongful act. The missing component is indemnification of the company for the wrongful acts of its directors and officers. Insurance companies can provide side "C" coverage to indemnify the company when it is named in a lawsuit. A public company can obtain coverage for securities claims only, whereas a private company gets full entity coverage. Often the company is also named in the suit, so this coverage is critical.

2. Definitions

Many risk managers, company representatives, and directors and officers can be confused when reading the insurance policy. To eliminate this confusion, we define below some terms found in D&O insurance policies:

- *Claim* means any judicial or administrative proceeding initiated against a director or officer in which he or she may be subject to a binding adjudication of liability for damages or other relief, including any appeal therefrom.
- *Wrongful act* means any error, misstatement, misleading statement, act, omission, neglect, or breach of duty committed, attempted, or allegedly committed or attempted by an insured person, individually or otherwise, in his insured capacity, or any matter claimed against him solely by reason of his serving in such insured capacity.

- *Loss* means damages, settlements and costs, charges, and expenses incurred by any of the directors and officers, but it does not include:
  - — Punitive or exemplary damages or that portion of any multiplied damage award that exceeds the amount multiplied.
  - — Taxes, criminal or civil fines, or penalties imposed by law.
  - — Matters deemed uninsurable under the law pursuant to which the policy shall be constructed.
- *Insured person* means any duly elected director of the corporation, including officer positions held by such directors, employees, or other members of management committees. Coverage applies to past, present, and future directors and officers. Covering former directors and officers is important because claims may involve incidents when such persons were actively associated with the named insured company. In covering future directors, the policy makes it clear that protection also applies to claims arising later, after new officers and directors have been elected. Generally, the D&O liability policy covers "wrongful acts" of elected directors and officers.
- *Policy year* means a period of one year following the effective date and hour of the policy or any anniversary thereof, or, if the time between the effective date or anniversary and the termination of the policy is less than one year, then that lesser period.
- *Subsidiary company,* as defined in several of the D&O liability forms, means any company wholly owned by the company named as the insured in the declarations, or any company of which the insured company owns more than 50% of the voting stock.

3. Common Exclusions

Due to the lack of uniformity among D&O insurance policies, it is important to review the exclusions and the potential risk to the organization. Listed below are some of the more basic exclusions relating to D&O liability arising out of wrongful acts. Typically, there is no coverage for claims involving:

- Any claim arising from invasion of privacy, wrongful entry, eviction, false arrest, false imprisonment, malicious prosecution, libel, or slander.
- The gain of any personal profit or advantage to which the insured was not legally entitled.
- The insured's return of any remuneration paid to the insured without the previous approval of the stockholders of the company named in the declarations (when a court has held such unapproved payments to be illegal).
- Dishonesty of the insured brought about, or contributed to, by the fraudulent act or omission or any criminal act or omission.
- Pollution and contamination caused by seepage, pollution, or contamination, or the cost of removing, nullifying, or cleaning up seeping, polluting, or contaminating substances.
- Any failure or omission on the part of the insured to secure and maintain insurance.
- A loss that is insured by any other existing valid policy or policies.
- Other public policy exclusions such as insider trading, discrimination in employment, violations of state and or federal laws, or monopolistic activities.
- Any loss or expense that is reimbursed by the company, when that reimbursement is a lawful obligation.
- Bodily injury, sickness, disease or death of any person, or damage to or destruction of any tangible property, including loss of use of it.
- Payments of monetary or non-monetary favors to foreign or domestic governments (including political contributions) and for similar payments to officers, directors, agents, owners, partners, representatives, or employees of any customers of the company.
- Any claim brought by any other insureds against one or more directors or officers or for wrongful termination of employment.
- Any offer to purchase, or purchase of, securities of the company at a premium over their current market value, made by the company or by the directors and officers.

- Any actual or alleged violation of the Racketeer Influenced and Corrupt Organizations (RICO) Act.
- Violation of any responsibilities, obligations, or duties imposed by the Employee Retirement Income Security Act of 1974 (ERISA).
- An insured vs. insured exclusion for suits brought by the insured organization against its directors and officers. The exclusion is designed to eliminate claims arising from in-fighting between the corporation and its senior management.
- Severability of exclusions: no conduct of any insured person shall be imputed to any other insured person to determine the application of any of the exclusions set forth in the policy.

4. Limit of Liability

A challenge when securing a D&O policy is deciding what limit is needed for the involved parties. Policies are customarily written subject to a combined single aggregate limit applying to losses paid under one of the policy's three insuring agreements. Many policies also combine other risks under a single limit or split limit such as employment practices liability insurance for employee-related issues. However, the limit may be eroded in the event that a company has a D&O claim and an employment-related claim covered under the same policy limit. An analysis should be done to determine whether defense costs should be inside or outside of the policy limits. D&O insurance policies typically include defense costs within the policy limits, meaning that the expenditure of defense costs reduces the policy's limit of liability. Since many D&O lawsuits involve highly complex areas of commercial and civil law, they are among the most expensive legal actions to defend. Consequently, limits should be selected to cover not only potential judgments and settlements but also anticipated defense costs.

5. General or Other Conditions

- *Cancellation:* The insurance company can notify the named insured company with a written cancellation notice; however, specific notices do not need to be sent to individual directors and officers.

Generally, cancellation for other than non-payment of premium requires a minimum of 30 days' notice, with many policies providing 60 days' notice.

- *Discovery option:* If the insurance company cancels or refuses to renew the policy, the insured may extend the policy for a period of 90 days upon payment of 50% of the annual premium. Extending the policy into the discovery period will not increase the limits from the previous policy year or extend the coverage for wrongful acts committed after the policy period.
- *Dispute resolution:* Due to the complexity and lack of conformity of D&O insurance policies, disputes between the insured and insurer can be common. Due to the possibility of disputes, insurers are beginning to build in alternative dispute resolution (ADR) provisions.
- *Run-off coverage:* If the policy is cancelled for merger, consolidation, or acquisition of a company or some other circumstance, a run-off policy will be secured. The run-off policy will cover wrongful acts taking place before the termination of the policy for a stipulated period of time.

Fiduciary Liability Coverage

There is potential liability for various officers of an organization as well as other persons acting in some capacity relating to an employer's pension, savings, profit-sharing, employee benefit, and health and welfare plans. People employed to design and administer such pension and employee benefit plans, including the management of the assets and liabilities of the plans, are liable to the plan beneficiaries for any breach of fiduciary duties. Therefore, fiduciary liability insurance is available and provides coverage, on behalf of the named insured, for legal liability arising from claims for alleged failure to prudently act within the meaning of the Employee Retirement Income Security Act of 1974 (ERISA).

The Definition and Duties of a Fiduciary

A fiduciary is someone who has undertaken to act for and on behalf of another in a particular matter in circumstances that give rise to a relationship of trust and confidence. Within the business setting, this could be a person who manages a retirement plan such as a 401(k), ESOP, SEP, defined benefit plan, or other such retirement plan. A fiduciary can also be involved with the administration of employee benefits such as health, dental, and disability insurance, as well as COBRA administration. Fiduciaries can be employees of a company who administer the employee benefits plan or outside service providers that may include investment advisors, actuarial consultants, accounting firms, and bank trust departments. The fiduciary, whether an employee or an outside service provider, must conform to the highest ethical standards when conducting his or her duties. These standards are higher than what is enforced under common law because ERISA requires the fiduciary to perform at a level of care and skill of a person who has expertise in fiduciary matters.

ERISA

ERISA establishes minimum standards for pension plans in private industry. It was enacted to protect the interests of employee benefit plan participants and their beneficiaries by requiring the disclosure of financial and other information concerning the plan, establishing standards of conduct for plan fiduciaries, and providing for appropriate remedies and access to the federal courts. Due to the obligations ERISA imposes on plan fiduciaries, it is imperative that such fiduciaries obtain insurance and/or bonding protection.

Fiduciary Considerations for an ESOP

Generally speaking, ERISA governs all health and retirement plans, including ESOPs. What is different about ESOPs versus other plans is the lack of diversification due to company stock being the primary and sometimes the only investment in an ESOP. Due to this concentration in company stock, ESOP fiduciaries must:

- Carefully select outside, independent service providers and require indemnification for their responsibilities. Remember that co-fiduciaries must have their own errors and omissions policy and the company cannot be indemnified under their policy.

- Arrange for independent, accurate stock valuations at least annually, keeping in mind that the fiduciary is ultimately responsible for evaluating and, if necessary, challenging the valuation to make sure it is for fair market value (or less, if buying shares from an outside shareholder).
- Evaluate the impact of buying and selling employer securities and its effect on remaining stockholders, particularly in regard to fairness with respect to the ESOP.
- Strictly abide by plan documents and the law.
- Avoid using plan assets to benefit key individuals.
- Consider the impact of ESOP post-transaction price decreases.
- Act as a responsible shareholder to prevent the wasting of corporate assets, such as excessive executive pay, and to vote the shares in accordance with plan documents and legal requirements.
- Purchase adequate fiduciary liability insurance.
- Assure timely compliance with reporting requirements and processing of employee complaints.
- Provide employees with necessary documentation, including annual account statements, and provide access, when requested, to required plan documents.

Fiduciary Insurance Policy

A fiduciary insurance policy is a non-standard insurance policy. Because the policies are unique, it is advisable to have fiduciary policies reviewed by trusted advisors and legal counsel to determine the coverage limit needed and discuss the exclusions under a typical policy. To have an insurance policy respond to a loss, one must first understand what a loss is and how it is defined. A loss is defined as "a wrongful act" that consists of a breach of fiduciary duty specified under ERISA that results in monetary damage to a plan participant. Many fiduciary policies also include specific policy language to include coverage for administrative errors and omissions associated with the management of pension or benefit plans. Costs associated with a wrongful act or omission could include legal fees, judgments, and interest payments.

Fiduciary Policy Exclusions

Exclusions vary among insurance policies and companies, so it is important to obtain the broadest policy possible with very specific exclusions listed with the policy. Some of the exclusions you will see are:

- Contractual liability that holds outside service providers harmless in the event of a loss.
- Criminal acts, including fraud and illegal profiteering.
- Punitive damages in excess of the actual loss sustained meant to punish the fiduciary.
- Known events of wrongdoing that occurred before the inception of the policy.

Fiduciary Policy vs. Fiduciary Bond

Confusion might arise with businesses as to the difference between the fiduciary liability policy and a fiduciary (ERISA) bond. As noted above, a fiduciary liability policy protects the personal assets of a plan fiduciary due to allegations of a breach of fiduciary duties under ERISA. The ERISA bond is posted to reimburse the plan for losses due to employee dishonesty in the amount of $500,000 or 10% of all plan assets, whichever is less. The Department of Labor has the authority to prescribe a bond in excess of $500,000, up to 10% of the value of all plan assets, as of the beginning of the plan year. As outlined above, a fiduciary liability policy protects the personal assets of a plan fiduciary due to allegations of a breach of fiduciary duties under ERISA.

Conclusion

The best risk-management practice is to abide by the duties of a director and officer to follow the duty of care or due diligence, the duty of loyalty, and the duty of obedience. With the responsibility of leadership, a director, officer, or fiduciary must always act in the best interests of its employees, stockholders, and stakeholders. Following the implementation of the above-listed duties, a company representative should carefully consider the purchase of D&O insurance and fiduciary insurance to safeguard the assets of the individual director and officer, fiduciary, and company. A company should contact its trusted advisors (including legal counsel and insurance agents) for a complete and thorough review of the necessary coverages for directors, officers, and fiduciaries.

Bibliography

ACE Directors and Officers Policy. MPDOOO. February 1999,

AIG PrivateEdge Directors and Officers Policy 68462. August 1997.

Chubb Private Company Risk Survey 2005.

Chubb ForeFront Portfolio Directors and Officers Policy 14-02-3796.

D&O Maps (Market Analysis and Policy Comparison Service) (online reference at www.irmi.com).

Great American ExecPro Directors and Officers Policy D2100. January 1999.

Hartford Directors and Officers Policy DO OOR291. June 1996.

IRMI, Directors and Officers Liability Policy Comparison Chart, December 1, 2007.

Travelers Wrap+ Directors and Officers Policy PDO-3001. July 2005.

"Trustees and Fiduciaries Liability Insurance." *Rough Notes,* December 2007.

CHAPTER 5

ESOP Basics for Board Members

Scott Rodrick
Corey Rosen

ESOPs have been around since the 1950s, when San Francisco attorney and investment banker Louis Kelso created the plans as a way to address what he saw as the growing gap between the minority of people who owned capital and the vast majority who owned little or none. Kelso was concerned that a changing economy would mean that returns to labor would start to stagnate or even shrink while returns to capital grew quickly, creating a gap between the wealthy few and everyone else that would be neither economically nor socially sustainable. Kelso did not believe that redistributive policies were the answer. Instead, he created a way to provide incentives for owners of businesses to share ownership with the people who worked for them.

The early ESOPs had to be approved one-by-one by the IRS. Finally, in 1974, after years of lobbying by Kelso, ESOPs were given statutory blessing by being made part of the Employee Retirement Income Security Act (ERISA), a new law designed to reform retirement, health, and other employee benefit plans. In theory, ESOPs could have been fit under some other statutory framework, but ERISA made sense in a number of ways, even if there were some areas that were awkward fits.

The fact that ESOPs became part of ERISA is significant in understanding how these plans work. Companies sponsoring ERISA plans receive tax benefits, as do their employees. In return for these benefits, the plans must be operated for the "exclusive benefit of plan participants" and must be nondiscriminatory, a term that has been defined primarily as not providing excessive benefits to highly compensated employees or unreasonably excluding employees from coverage. All

ERISA retirement plans operate through a trustee overseen by a plan fiduciary who is responsible to see that the plans comply with the law and plan documents. The fiduciaries can be sued by participants and/or the government for failing to do so.

The essential concept of ESOPs under ERISA is that Congress will allow companies to use pretax dollars to fund a plan to buy company stock (principal and interest), including when the plan borrows money to do so. Employees, in turn, pay no tax on the benefit until it is actually distributed to them. Congress added additional benefits for sellers later on, and even more benefits for S corporations. These benefits are striking. There is no other way for companies to use pretax dollars to buy their own shares, to use pretax dollars to repay the principal on corporate debt, or for retirement plans to buy company stock without meeting more rigorous fiduciary requirements concerning asset diversification. Moreover, no other retirement plan can borrow money to buy company stock.

Since their statutory blessing in 1974, ESOPs have grown from a few hundred plans to about 11,000 plans covering about 11 million employees with over $900 billion in assets (as of 2009). As they have matured, more ESOP companies are now 100% ESOP-owned. They are often seen as not just transitional vehicles to buy out one or more owners only to sell the company down the road. Instead, they are increasingly seen as defining aspects of corporate identity and are expected to be part of the company's long-term future. Largely as a result of this, ESOP companies have become more serious about their governance arrangements.

As an ESOP board member, you do not have to be an expert on ESOP law and practice. But it is essential that you know the basic concepts and best practices. This chapter looks as three primary issues:

- How ESOPs work
- The role of the ESOP fiduciary compared to ESOP board members
- ESOPs and corporate culture

ESOP Basics

Plan Structure

To create an ESOP, companies set up an employee stock ownership trust. The trust is governed by a trustee appointed by the board. This can be an independent outside firm (about 22% of ESOPs) or one or more insiders, although sellers to an ESOP should not be trustees because of potential conflict of interest situations. The company funds the plan by making contributions on a regular basis. These are then allocated to plan participants as they are made, are subject to vesting, and then are paid after employees terminate or when they are provided with diversification options before termination.

While the trustee is formally in charge of the ESOP, if anyone or any entity causes the trustee to take an action, whether directly or by providing insufficient or misleading information, that individual or entity becomes a plan fiduciary as well. If challenged by court or by audit, the plan fiduciaries, regardless of titles, are the ones at risk.

Tax Incentives for ESOPs

Corporate Incentives

Up to 25% of covered compensation[1] can be contributed on a deductible basis in all ESOPs, whether in a C corporation or an S corporation and whether the ESOP is leveraged or not. All contributions of a C corporation to pay interest on a leveraged ESOP's loan are deductible over and above the 25% amount. For S corporations, however, interest payments are included in the 25% limit. In C corporations, contributions made to the ESOP but not used to pay ESOP debt and

1. Covered compensation is the eligible compensation of all employees in the plan, excluding pay for any individual over $245,000 (as of 2009; this figure is indexed for inflation yearly). Generally, W-2 compensation is used to calculate eligible compensation, but some companies may place additional limits on what is counted as pay (such as a $100,000 cap or not counting certain bonuses or commissions). In addition, if the seller to an ESOP takes a tax deferral on the gain under Section 1042 of the Internal Revenue Code, the seller, direct relatives of the seller, and more-than-25% owners cannot receive an allocation of shares through the ESOP, and thus their pay is also not counted as eligible except for the purpose of cash contributions to the plan.

contributions to other defined contribution plans do not count toward this 25%-of-pay limit, but they do in S corporations.

In C companies, employers can deduct dividends that are paid on ESOP-held stock if used to pay ESOP debt, are passed through to employees, or are voluntarily reinvested in the company by plan participants. Dividend deductions are not subject to the 25% limits described above for ESOP contributions. To be deductible, dividends must be "reasonable"; additionally, they are not deducted from income when computing the alternative minimum tax. Dividends are not deductible in the case of S corporation ESOPs, but S corporation distributions can be used to repay ESOP debt.

S corporations with ESOPs have a major, and unique, advantage, however. Any corporate profits attributable to the ESOP are not subject to income tax. If an ESOP owns 30% of an S corporation, for example, it does not pay tax on that 30% of the profits. Although profits in an S corporation are passed through and taxed to the owners instead of being paid by the company, S corporations generally end up paying distributions to the owners to fund their tax bills, so, in practice, the ESOP's tax advantage becomes the S corporation's tax advantage. When an S corporation is 100% owned by its ESOP, there is no income tax at all to pay. (This is true for federal taxes; most states track the federal rules and offer the same tax exclusion.) S ESOPs must, however, receive a pro-rata share of any distributions made to owners, even though the ESOP has no tax obligation.

The ability to avoid tax, predictably, lured a lot of people into ESOPs who had not the least interest in providing benefits to employees but did have a lot of interest in avoiding taxes for a few key people. A variety of schemes were created and aggressively marketed, from one-person ESOPs to complex arrangements with management companies separated from operating companies, elaborate deferred compensation arrangements, multiple subsidiaries, and more. Equally predictably, Congress (with the strong support of the ESOP community) cracked down on these abusive plans. The result was a fairly complex law with a very simple organizing concept: the benefits of an ESOP in an S corporation must be provided broadly to employees, not excessively concentrated in a few hands. Essentially, companies have to calculate how much ownership people have, whether in the ESOP directly, or through synthetic equity (such as options, phantom stock, stock appreciation rights, or other long-term incentives). If people who individually own more than 10% of all the ownership attributable to the ESOP or synthetic equity (or 20% for family members) collectively own more than 50% of all the equity (counting not only the ESOP and synthetic equity but also direct ownership and ownership that is attributed to them), then there are draconian tax consequences. These are not difficult tests to meet if the ESOP is genuinely broad-based, and provide considerable latitude for executive incentives, but plan administrators need to monitor compliance regularly to avoid potential problems.

Seller Incentives

An owner of a closely held C corporation (but not an S corporation) can defer capital gains taxation on stock he or she sells to an ESOP if (1) the ESOP owns 30% or more of each class of outstanding stock or of the total value of all outstanding stock, excluding nonconvertible, nonvoting preferred stock; and (2) the seller reinvests ("rolls over") the sales proceeds into qualified replacement property (stocks or bonds of domestic operating companies) during the period from three months before to twelve months after the sale. None of the shares sold to the ESOP in a transaction to which section 1042 applies may be allocated to ESOP accounts of the seller, certain relatives of the seller (ancestors, siblings, the spouse, or lineal descendants), non-selling shareholders holding more than 25% of company stock, or family members of the more-than-25% shareholders if they own stock by attribution (e.g., spouses). The selling shareholder(s) must have held the stock for at least three years before the sale and cannot have received the stock through exercising stock options or other stock awards for which the employee did not pay fair market value.

Employee Benefits and Taxation

Employees pay no tax on stock allocated to their ESOP accounts until they receive distributions; at that point, they are taxed on the distributions. The portion that is attributable to corporate contributions is taxed as ordinary income; gains on the stock are taxed as capital gains. If employees are younger than age 59½ (or age 55 if they have terminated employment), they, like employees in qualified plans generally, are subject not only to applicable taxes but also to an additional 10% excise tax on the ordinary income part of the distribution unless they roll the money over into an IRA or a successor plan in another company (or unless the participant terminates employment due to death or disability).

If the money is rolled over into an IRA or successor plan, the employee pays no tax until the money is withdrawn, at which point it is taxed as ordinary income. Rollovers from ESOP distributions to IRAs are available for distributions of stock or cash over periods of less than 10 years.

When dividends are directly paid to plan participants on the stock allocated to their ESOP accounts, they are fully taxable, although they are exempt from income tax withholding and are not subject to the excise tax that applies to early distributions.

ESOP Requirements

Annual Additions

There are limits on how much can be added to individual employee accounts each year. The combination of employer contributions and employee deferrals for defined contribution plans (ESOPs, 401(k) plans, etc.) into the account of any given individual plan participant cannot exceed the lesser of (1) 100% of the participant's pay or (2) $49,000 (as of 2009; this dollar limit is indexed yearly for inflation). Employees can defer up to $15,500 to their 401(k) plans (as of 2009; again, this is indexed yearly for inflation). Employees aged 50 and over can add $5,500 more to the 401(k) limit (as of 2009; these additional amounts, called "catch-up contributions," are indexed for inflation). In a C corporation, but not an S corporation, neither forfeitures of unvested allocations nor dividends count toward the contribution limits, provided not more than one-third of the ESOP benefits are allocated to highly compensated employees. In S corporations, company distributions (which are not technically dividends and are not tax-deductible) do not count as contributions and are not covered by the 25%-of-pay limit. These S corporation distributions, when made to either allocated or unallocated shares, can be used to repay an ESOP loan without limit.

Coverage

An ESOP is by its nature a broad-based program, and usually all full-time employees aged 21 or over with at least one year of service participate. The following groups of employees may be excluded: (1) nonresident aliens; (2) employees in a separate line of business with 50 or more employees; and (3) employees covered by collective bargaining agreements, provided that retirement benefits have been the subject of good-faith collective bargaining. In addition, other available tests can be used to qualify, although the large majority of ESOPs do not need to rely on them.

Allocations of ESOP Shares

Shares must be allocated among participants based on their relative compensation or some other formula that does not discriminate in favor of highly compensated employees. There are restrictions on family members and more-than-25% owners on receiving allocations of stock where the seller has deferred capital gains tax on the sale of those shares by reinvesting in other companies.

Vesting and Forfeitures

Employees who leave the company before becoming fully vested will forfeit their benefits to the extent they are not vested in them. An employee must become 100% vested when he or she reaches "normal retirement age" as defined in the Code. Additionally, an ESOP must comply with one of the following two minimum schedules for vesting (plans may provide different standards if they are more generous to participants):

- No vesting at all in the first years, followed by a sudden 100% vesting after not more than three years of service ("cliff" vesting); or
- Twenty percent vesting after the second year of service, with 20% more each year until 100% vesting occurs after the sixth year of service ("graded" vesting).

A "year of service" generally refers to a plan year in which a participant has 1,000 hours of service; it may include past service.

When departing employees leave before they are fully vested in their accounts, the amount that is not vested is forfeited; it is usually reallocated to remaining participants and may limit the amount of other contributions that can be allocated to such participants. Forfeitures may be used for administrative costs in rare situations.

If ESOP contributions are designated as an employer match in a 401(k) plan, then contributions designed to meet the 401(k) safe harbor tests must vest immediately, as with any contributions designed to meet those tests.

Diversification

After ESOP participants reach age 55 and have participated in the plan for ten years, they have the right during the following five years to diversify up to a total of 25% of company stock that was acquired by the ESOP after December 31, 1986, and has been allocated to their accounts; during the sixth year, they may diversify up to a total of 50%, minus any previously diversified shares. To satisfy the diversification requirement, the ESOP must (1) offer at least three alternative investments under either the ESOP or another plan such as a 401(k) plan, or (2) distribute cash or company stock to the participants.

Anti-cutback Rules

Under "anti-cutback" rules that apply to qualified plans such as ESOPs, accrued benefits cannot be reduced or eliminated except under certain conditions. With ESOPs, there are circumstances under which benefits in cash may be substituted for distributions in stock and under which the timing and form of distributions may be changed in a nondiscriminatory manner.

Distributions After Leaving Employment

The special rules for ESOP distributions provide that when a participant retires, becomes disabled, or dies, the ESOP must begin to distribute vested benefits during the plan year following the event. When employment terminates for other reasons, such as when an employee quits, distribution must start no later than the sixth plan year after the plan year in which termination occurred (unless the participant is re-employed by the same company before then). However, if the ESOP is leveraged and in a C corporation, distributions of shares acquired through the loan generally may be delayed until the plan year after the plan year in which the ESOP loan is fully repaid (it is unclear whether S corporations can do this).

Under the special ESOP rules, distributions may be made in a lump sum or in substantially equal payments (not less frequently than annually) over a period no longer than five years (i.e., six payments over five years). Distributions are made in the form of cash or stock.

Regardless of the special ESOP rules, the general qualified retirement plan rules provide that a plan must (unless the participant chooses otherwise) begin distributing benefits no later than the 60th day after the end of the plan year in which the latest of the following events occurs: (1) the participant attains age 65 or the plan's normal retirement age, whichever comes first; (2) the participant reaches the 10th anniversary of participation in the plan; or (3) termination of service. Additionally, there are rules governing distributions after death. Where the special ESOP rules and the general retirement plan rules conflict, the rule that produces an earlier distribution prevails.

Put Option

Closely held companies that sponsor an ESOP must provide a "put option" on company stock distributed to participants by allowing them to sell the stock back to the company at its current fair market value. At a minimum, the put option must be available during two periods, one for at least 60 days immediately following distribution and one for at least 60 days during the following plan year.

Privately held banks that are prohibited from buying their own securities can avoid providing a put option if participants can take distributions in cash.

Restrictions on Transferring Stock

Participants generally can sell company stock they receive from the ESOP to anyone, except that the plan may provide that the employer and the ESOP have rights of first refusal to match any offer received from a third party for such stock.

However, if the employer is a closely held company whose charter or bylaws restrict the ownership of substantially all (approximately 85%) of its stock to employees or a qualified plan, or if the employer is an S corporation, the ESOP (if the plan so provides) is not required to distribute stock; instead, it can distribute cash, or the employer can require the employee to sell distributed stock back to the employer.

The Rights of ESOP Participants

Voting

The ESOP fiduciary votes the ESOP shares. Closely held companies generally only need to give participants voting rights regarding a merger or consolidation, recapitalization, reclassification, liquidation, dissolution, or sale of substantially all of the assets of a trade or business of the company. The plan may either give participants the right to direct how the shares allocated to their accounts are voted or specify a one-vote-per-participant arrangement. These issues do not necessarily include the sale of stock, including all of a company's shares. Companies can voluntarily pass through additional rights. Otherwise, the plan trustee votes the shares.

Information Rights

The employer must give plan participants a summary description of the plan, a summary annual report of the plan, individual benefit statements on request, access to plan documents, and information on issues subject to voting by participants.

Claims and Legal Actions

If a participant's claim for ESOP benefits is denied, the employer or the plan must provide a written explanation and the opportunity for a review of the decision.

Participants and beneficiaries may file complaints in federal court for improper conduct, as when an ESOP has paid the selling shareholders too much for stock, thus leaving the participants with fewer shares than they deserve. Other common grounds for litigation involving ESOPs include the denial of benefits, a failure to abide by the rules of a plan (such as not distributing shares at the required time), the conversion of profit sharing assets into an ESOP of a company that subsequently does poorly, a cutback in promised benefits, and takeover-related issues.

Valuation Issues

The law requires an independent, outside appraisal for ESOPs. Independence has been interpreted to mean that the appraiser can have no other business relationship with the ESOP company.

Anyone can claim to be in the business of doing ESOP appraisals. There are no certification programs and no specific required credentials. Many appraisers do have some kind of credentialing from the American Society of Appraisers (ASA), the American Institute of Certified Public Accountants (AICPA), or another national accounting organization. There are many designations, and appraisers do not agree on which are the most useful. It is important to ask the appraiser specifically what the credentials required. Was there a rigorous course? A test to pass?

Approaches to Enterprise Value

The first step in an appraisal is to calculate enterprise value—how much the entire business is worth, as opposed to how much an individual share is worth. Three approaches are almost always considered:

- *Comparable companies:* The appraiser will look for similar companies to find what they have sold for and what their key ratios are for such things as share price relative to earnings or free cash flow. The best data are from public companies, but these may not be comparable to your company because of size, capitalization, diversification, and other factors. Data on sales of comparable companies may not always be reliable or sufficient, and truly comparable companies may be hard to find.
- *Income:* The most heavily weighted of the three approaches to valuation is usually based on a measure of income: appraisers often

use capitalization of historical cash flow, discounted projected cash flows, or a combination thereof. There are many ways to measure earnings or cash flow, such as EBITDA (earnings before interest, taxes, depreciation, and amortization). An appraiser will use one or more measures considered appropriate for the particular business, then look to financial markets to calculate how much a willing buyer would pay a willing seller for the right to these earnings or cash flows given the level of risk in your particular company. Calculations of future earnings or cash flow are based on past performance and management projections of future performance. Appraisers, of course, should not simply accept these projections, but should rigorously question just how apt they are. Historical earnings or cash flow will be normalized to adjust for unusual factors, such as excessive (or very low) executive or other employee pay or perquisites, one-time events (such as a lawsuit settlement), excess capacity, etc.

- *Asset value:* A company's liquidation value is a factor in valuation, but only if the company is worth more dead than alive. On the other hand, a company may have non-performing or underperforming assets, such as real estate not used for the business, or assets that could be better deployed (such as an office in a prime area that could be sold and replaced with a less expensive one without hurting the business). These assets may be added to the final value.

Generally, appraisers will weight all three approaches, usually putting the most emphasis on the second. Appraisal reports should provide very detailed explanations of how and why these weightings were done. Although different appraisers may use different weightings, they may end up in much the same place.

Adjustments to Enterprise Value

All of this is standard valuation procedure likely to be used in any business appraisal. In ESOPs, several additional factors come up as well.

Liquidity discounts reflect how difficult or easy it is to sell a share. Public company stock has near perfect liquidity; most closely held stock is highly illiquid. Most appraisers put ESOPs somewhere in between, arguing that the ESOP provides liquidity, albeit not as readily as a public market. As we noted earlier, there is some disagreement about whether the put right for participants that provides this liquidity really can be considered (although most appraisers do). But even if it is, it is hard to argue that a right that can only be exercised pursuant to termination or diversification, and then only in selected windows, has the same liquidity as a public company share. Liquidity discounts range anywhere from zero (although we would argue this is a very hard position to sustain) to around 35%.

Many appraisers also reflect the repurchase obligation through the liquidity discount. The argument here is that if the ESOP company has a good record of buying back the shares, and has adequate resources to handle future obligations, then the liquidity discount would be low; if not, it should be high. Other appraisers factor in repurchase through any projected reduction in future earnings required to handle the repurchases. It is essential for plan fiduciaries to make sure that they have carefully considered these issues and chosen a course that is in the best long-term interests of participants. If the appraiser is too aggressive in ignoring or downplaying the effect of the repurchase obligation, the company's ability to buy out future participants is jeopardized, sometimes forcing an unwanted sale. Even if that does not happen, by paying too much for shares now, the company effectively punishes those very employees who stay around longer to build value, while depriving the company of cash that can be used to grow the business.

A second discount applies for a lack of control. Owning a minority interest is worth less per share than owning a controlling interest. Owning control allows the owner to make decisions about the use of assets, and that right carries a price. When public companies receive unsolicited offers, the share price often goes up significantly because the acquirer is buying control from the company's shareholders, all of whom, with rare exceptions, are minority owners. In closely held companies, lack-of-control discounts often range from 20% to 40%. Control is not simply an either-or status, however. Certain shareholder rights may require supermajority levels, for instance, while even minority owners may acquire some rights if they own a large enough minority. As a result, there may be different discounts for different levels of control.

As we discussed earlier, ESOPs often buy stock in stages. Whether they can then pay for control throughout is a controversial issue. At the least, however, ESOPs should be able to pay for control only if they have control rights, no matter what their ownership level, and a guarantee for financing to buy the next level of control. A similar issue is whether the ESOP should pay a control price for buying additional shares when it already has control (going from 60% to 80%, for instance). Opinions are divided here as well.

Boards and Fiduciaries

Plan fiduciaries must protect the interest of plan participants as plan participants, not as employees. That means that they must operate the plan to maximize the long-term value of plan assets. The trustee is also the shareholder and must act to protect the interest of the assets of the trust as any other major shareholder would.

While trustees are formally responsible for the plan, anyone who causes the plan to make a decision (such as by directing the trustee) becomes a plan fiduciary responsible for all the requirements of the plan and the law. Even if a board does not in any way direct the fiduciary, it still has an ERISA fiduciary obligation to use appropriate care and judgment in selecting an appropriate trustee and monitoring the trustee's actions to make sure it follows the requirements of the plan and the law. This does not mean board members have to review every decision in detail, but it does mean that they must have enough communication with the trustees to feel confident that decisions are being made properly and with the appropriate information.

The key issues where trustees' and board members' interests overlap include the following.

Making Sure That the ESOP Pays the Right Price

The ESOP cannot pay more than fair market value when buying shares from an owner, although it can negotiate for a lower price. When buying shares from departing employees, it should pay fair market value. Trustees (or anyone acting as a fiduciary in this matter) should not simply accept what an appraiser concludes. They must carefully evaluate the appraisal report, making sure the assumptions are legitimate and the information received is adequate and accurate.

In contrast, boards might agree that the company can directly pay a shareholder more than fair market value for shares if this is not construed as wasting corporate assets. For instance, the board might authorize the company to pay more to an owner who has acted as an executive to compensate for lower-than-normal salary, to make a larger transaction possible, to buy out a minority owner so the ESOP could go to 100% status and convert to an S corporation, or for other reasons that clearly benefit shareholders overall.

Making Sure Plan Rules and the Law Are Followed

The trustee must ensure that fees are reasonable and that allocations, vesting, distributions, voting rights, information rights, government filings, and other administrative matters are handled properly. Boards generally do not have much involvement in this part of the trustee's work unless there appear to be problems. Instead, the key issue for boards is to monitor the trustee by asking for periodic reports on how it is making sure these issues are being properly addressed (often, this will be primarily by hiring well-qualified plan administrators).

Responding to Offers

The area of greatest potential conflict is responding to offers. Companies normally receive many offers from brokers (or sometimes competitors) that are sent to multiple companies in their field and that are more fishing expeditions than serious inquiries. ESOP company boards normally ignore them. When an attractive offer is made that appears to be adequately financed and specified, however, the board is obliged by corporate law to give it consideration. Company bylaws and state corporate laws may give boards some leeway in deciding what to do. In addition to considering whether their owners want to sell at all, they may be able to consider such matters as corporate values, keeping the company local, or retaining employment, to name the most common.

An ESOP trustee (or fiduciary, if not solely the trustee), however, has a different perspective. The law requires the fiduciary to accept any offer that significantly enhances the long-term value of plan assets. This does not mean the fiduciary simply should say yes to any higher offer. The financial structure and certainty of the offer need to be assessed first, but even if they are solid, the fiduciary might conclude that in the long term, the employees would be better off if the offer were rejected. This could be because the fiduciary believes a better offer might be made later, that the value of company stock will increase quickly enough as a stand-alone company to make the long-term value greater, or because the future planned contributions to the ESOP will be much greater than what employees would get under the acquirer's plans.

Procedurally, the board must pass on any legitimate offers to the fiduciary for review. If the fiduciary wants to pursue the offer, the board should cooperate in that effort. In some cases, the law or plan documents will require that employees vote on the sale (this is always true if the sale is sale of all or substantially all the assets), although the fiduciary could override that decision in some unusual cases.

The reality has been that fiduciary-board conflicts over proposed offers are extremely rare. ESOP companies that do not want to be sold do not make the most appealing targets because of all the procedural hoops they require. If the board does favor a sale, the fiduciary (and the employees) are usually happy to go along because there is a very attractive offer.

Executive Compensation

This is a primary area of board focus, of course. The ESOP trustee (or fiduciary causing the trustee to make a decision) should act as a responsible shareholder to make sure this compensation does not constitute a wasting of corporate assets by paying executives well above what can be justified by their contributions to the company. Trustees must also assure that deferred compensation plans offered to executives, such as stock appreciation rights, phantom stock, stock options, and other deferred incentives, are not so large as to trigger "anti-abuse" rules in S ESOP companies.

Sustainability of the ESOP

Another concern for the board may be to make the ESOP sustainable over time. A primary focus here is managing the obligation to buy back shares from former employees. This means making sure that adequate analyses are performed and financial plans made. In addition, boards should look at how new employees can become owners of shares in mature ESOPs. Often, there may be only a limited number of shares to make available at this point (mostly through recontributing or recycling shares from departing employees). If this is not adequate, then the board can consider alternatives such as "rebalancing" (having the plan structured so that shares from more senior people are replaced with cash contributed to the plan for that purpose, while the shares purchased from those sales go to newer employees), issuing more shares, or releveraging.

Trustees here are in a reactive mode, responding to these policies to make sure they protect employee owner interests. The trustee should, however, pay particular attention to the issue of whether the ESOP valuation is reflecting the liability created by the ongoing repurchase obligation to make sure the plan does not pay too much in the present at the risk of its future.

Culture

Many board members have told us that one of the issues that matter most to them is making sure the company has and sustains an ownership culture. This includes using open-book management practices, effective communications about how the ESOP works, and employee involvement in job-level decisions. The research on this is very clear: companies that do this perform much better. So while this may seem like a "soft" issue, in fact, it is critical to the success of the company. Boards can work with top leadership to make sure they are following through on these issues.

Defining Board, Trustee, and ESOP Committee Responsibilities

While there are areas where board and trustee duties intersect, there are many where they do not—or should not. If these responsibilities are not clearly delineated, board members may be subject to unintended fiduciary responsibility. The description below, taken from the article

"Designing and Drafting ESOPs" by Kevin Long,[2] serves as a useful quick reference.

A. The board shall have the authority on behalf of the corporation to:
   1. Adopt, amend and terminate the plan;
   2. Appoint and remove members of the administrative committee and appoint and remove the trustee(s); and
   3. Determine a funding policy and method for the plan and amounts of all contributions to the plan.

B. The committee shall have the authority in its sole discretion to:
   1. Allocate the company's contribution under the plan's terms;
   2. Establish rules pertaining to participants' optional investment accounts;
   3. Maintain pooled or separate accounts for participant benefits;
   4. Furnish, and correct errors in, statements of accounts;
   5. Determine the method, timing, and media of distributions, under the terms of the plan and direct the trustee(s) with respect to distributions;
   6. Approve distributions to beneficiaries;
   7. Direct the segregation of assets pursuant to the terms of the plan, but without discretion over the investment policy for the plan;
   8. Approve distribution of the interests of incompetent persons and minors;
   9. Construe the terms of the plan and trust document and determine all questions of interpretation and its application to determine participant benefits;
   10. Perform all record keeping and administrative functions necessary to comply with the reporting and filing requirements of the Code and ERISA; and

2. Kevin Long, "Designing and Drafting ESOPs," *Journal of Employee Ownership Law and Finance* 20, no. 3 (summer 2008): 65–66.

11. Employ advisors, agents, and counsel in fulfilling these duties.

C. The trustee(s) shall have the authority to:

1. Establish the fair market value of the trust fund including through the use of qualified independent appraisers;
2. Value segregated accounts;
3. Purchase and sell company stock or other plan assets and otherwise manage and invest trust assets. Hold the trust assets and render accounts of their administration of the trust;
5. Vote the trust's shares of the company if and as provided in the plan and consistent with ERISA;
6. Determine the amount of the trust's income or loss;
7. Appoint and delegate duties to an investment manager;
8. Determine the trust's investment policy, in light of the plan's funding policy and method; and
9. Employ advisors, agents, and counsel in fulfilling these duties.

Conclusion

As ESOPs have matured, more and more companies are creating and sustaining boards that play an active role in the company. Many of these boards have outside directors. This is an encouraging development that bodes well for the future success of ESOPs. ESOP board members who take their duties seriously can add significant value. While there are more issues for board members in ESOP companies to consider than in non-ESOP companies, there is also the considerable satisfaction of working in an environment where the fruits of that effort can result in a significant increase in the wealth of a broad group of people. Moreover, many ESOP companies are on the cutting edge of management and organizational culture innovation, making these companies exciting places for everyone to be.

About the Authors

Stephen P. Magowan is a shareholder in Steiker, Fischer, Edwards & Greenapple, P.C. and a member of SES Advisors, Inc. Steve's practice focuses on counseling privately held companies on ownership transition through ESOPs and employee-owned cooperatives and on counseling business owners and others on complex estate planning issues. Steve helped to found the Vermont Employee Ownership Center (VEOC) in 2001. He has lectured at each VEOC annual conference; at many other ESOP-related conferences, including the annual conferences of the National Center for Employee Ownership, the ESOP Association, and the New England chapter of the ESOP Association; and the Million Dollar Roundtable and Harris M. Plaisted annual conferences. Steve is a member of the Chittenden County, Vermont, and New York Bar Associations, as well as the American Bar Association. Steve has published many articles on tax planning issues for ESOP transactions and is the author of BNA Tax Management Portfolio no. 804, *Probate and Estate Administration.* Steve received his law degree from Washington University in Saint Louis, Missouri, and received his Bachelor of Arts with highest honors from Ohio University. In law school, Steve served as a research assistant to professors F. Hodge O'Neal and Robert Thompson to update their treatises *O'Neal's Oppression of Minority Shareholders* and *O'Neal's Close Corporations.* After completing law school, Steve clerked for Justice Henry R. Horsey of the Delaware Supreme Court.

Scott Rodrick is the director of publishing and information technology at the National Center for Employee Ownership (NCEO). He is an attorney and served at the U.S. Department of Labor as an attorney-advisor before coming to the NCEO. He designed and created the NCEO's present line of publications and is the author or coauthor of several books, including the NCEO's bestseller *An Introduction to ESOPs* (9th ed. 2008). He is the editor of the *Journal of Employee Ownership Law and Finance,* the only professional journal in the English language devoted to employee stock plans. Rodrick is also a Web developer. He created the NCEO's Web site in 1994 and has maintained and expanded it since then.

Corey Rosen is the executive director of the National Center for Employee Ownership (NCEO). He cofounded the NCEO in 1981 after working for five years as a professional staff member in the U.S. Senate, where he helped draft legislation on employee ownership plans. Before that, he taught political science at Ripon College. He is the author or coauthor of many books and over 100 articles on employee ownership, and coauthor (with John Case and Martin Staubus) of *Equity: Why Employee Ownership Is Good for Business* (Harvard Business School Press, 2005). He was the subject of an extensive interview in *Inc.* magazine in August 2000; has appeared frequently on CNN, PBS, NPR, and other network programs; and is regularly quoted in the *Wall Street Journal,* the *New York Times,* and other leading publications. He has a Ph.D. in political science from Cornell University and serves on the advisory board of the Certified Equity Professional Institute. He served on the board of directors of the Great Place to Work Institute, creator of *Fortune* magazine's "100 Best Companies to Work for in America" list. He also serves on the trustee committee for SWA Associates and on the board of Dealey Renton Associates, both ESOP companies.

John D. Schlichte is the president of the Presidio Group, located in Salt Lake City, Utah. He is a risk manager specializing in alternative risk financing. He is a Certified Risk Manager (CRM), Certified Insurance Counselor (CIC), and Certified WorkComp Advisor (CWCA) with over 15 years of experience.

Cecil Ursprung is a former employee-owner of Reflexite Corporation (1983–2009), where he served as CEO for 23 years. Reflexite is majority owned by its employees through its ESOP. In 1992, Mr. Ursprung and the 350 employee-owners of Reflexite Corporation were chosen as *Inc.* magazine's Entrepreneurs of the Year, and in 2007 the company was selected by the *Wall Street Journal* as one of the nation's 15 best small business employers. Mr. Ursprung serves on the boards of four companies (three private and one public), ranging in size from $20 million to $260 million in sales. He is vice president of government relations for the New England Chapter of the ESOP Association and is co-chair of the board of the National Center for Employee Ownership. His education includes a degree in economics and finance from Baylor University, an MBA from Washington University in St. Louis, Missouri, and postgraduate work at the University of Michigan. He is a frequent speaker on topics such as employee ownership, government relations, business strategy development, employee motivation, the effective use of outside boards, and executive compensation.

Michael Wade is vice president of the Presidio Group's surety department. He is a risk manager specializing in bonding and fiduciary insurance. He is a Certified Risk Manager (CRM) and Certified WorkComp Advisor (CWCA) with over seven years of experience.

About the NCEO

The National Center for Employee Ownership (NCEO) is widely considered to be the leading authority in employee ownership in the U.S. and the world. Established in 1981 as a nonprofit information and membership organization, it now has over 2,500 members, including companies, professionals, unions, government officials, academics, and interested individuals. It is funded entirely through the work it does.

The NCEO's mission is to provide the most objective, reliable information possible about employee ownership at the most affordable price possible. As part of the NCEO's commitment to providing objective information, it does not lobby or provide ongoing consulting services. The NCEO publishes a variety of materials on employee ownership and participation, holds dozens of seminars, Webinars, and conferences on employee ownership annually, and offers a variety of online courses. The NCEO's work includes extensive contacts with the media, both through articles written for trade and professional publications and through interviews with reporters. It has written or edited several books for outside publishers. The NCEO maintains an extensive Web site at www.nceo.org.

NCEO Membership Benefits

- The bimonthly newsletter *Employee Ownership Report,* which covers ESOPs, equity compensation, and employee participation.
- Access to the members-only area of the NCEO's Web site, which includes a searchable newsletter archive, a discussion forum, a database of service providers, and more.
- Substantial discounts on publications, online courses, and events produced by the NCEO.
- Free access to live Webinars and conference calls.
- The right to contact the NCEO for answers to general or specific questions regarding employee ownership.

An introductory NCEO membership costs $90 for one year ($100 outside the U.S.) and covers an entire company at all locations, a single professional offering services in this field, or a single individual with a business interest in employee ownership. Full-time students and faculty members who are not employed in the business sector may join at the academic rate of $40 for one year ($50 outside the U.S.).

Selected NCEO Publications

The NCEO offers a variety of publications on all aspects of employee ownership and participation. Below are some of our publications. To obtain the most current information on what we have available, visit us on the Web at www.nceo.org or call us at 510-208-1300.

Employee Stock Ownership Plans (ESOPs)

- *Understanding ESOPs* is an overview of the issues involved in establishing and operating an ESOP.

  $25 for NCEO members, $35 for nonmembers

- *S Corporation ESOPs* introduces the reader to how ESOPs work and then discusses the legal, valuation, administrative, and other issues associated with S corporation ESOPs.

  $25 for NCEO members, $35 for nonmembers

- *ESOP Valuation* brings together and updates where needed the best articles on ESOP valuation we have published in our journal.

  $25 for NCEO members, $35 for nonmembers

- *ESOPs and Corporate Governance* covers everything from shareholder rights to the impact of Sarbanes-Oxley to choosing a fiduciary.

  $25 for NCEO members, $35 for nonmembers

- *The ESOP Communications Sourcebook* provides ideas for and examples of communicating an ESOP to employees and customers. It includes a CD with communications materials, including many documents that readers can customize for their own companies.

  $35 for NCEO members, $50 for nonmembers

- *The ESOP Company Board Handbook* is a guide for board members in ESOP companies.

  $25 for NCEO members, $35 for nonmembers

- *The Inside ESOP Fiduciary Handbook* provides an overview of the issues involved in being a fiduciary at an ESOP company.

  $25 for NCEO members, $35 for nonmembers

- *How ESOP Companies Handle the Repurchase Obligation* has essays and recent research on the subject.

  $25 for NCEO members, $35 for nonmembers

- *Model ESOP* provides a sample ESOP plan, with alternative provisions given to tailor the plan to individual needs. It also includes a section-by-section explanation of the plan and other supporting materials.

  $50 for NCEO members, $75 for nonmembers

- *Administrative Issues for ESOP Companies* is a guide to the issues that arise in operating an ESOP, from filing Form 5500 to dealing with Internal Revenue Service or Department of Labor audits.

  $25 for NCEO members, $35 for nonmembers

- *Executive Compensation in ESOP Companies* discusses executive compensation issues, special ESOP considerations, and a survey of executive compensation in ESOP companies.

  $25 for NCEO members, $35 for nonmembers

- *Selling Your Business to an ESOP* is a guide for owners, managers, and advisors of closely held businesses, including details on the tax-deferred Section 1042 "rollover" for C corporation owners.

  $25 for NCEO members, $35 for nonmembers

- *Leveraged ESOPs and Employee Buyouts* discusses how ESOPs borrow money to buy out entire companies, purchase shares from a retiring owner, or finance new capital.

  $25 for NCEO members, $35 for nonmembers

- *Don't Do That* is a guide to common mistakes in operating an ESOP and what to do about them.

  $25 for NCEO members, $35 for nonmembers

- *The ESOP Committee Guide* is the definitive guide to creating, developing, and maintaining a successful ESOP committee.

  $25 for NCEO members, $35 for nonmembers

Equity Compensation

- *The Decision-Maker's Guide to Equity Compensation* describes the various types of equity compensation, how they work, and how to decide how much to give and to whom.

  $25 for NCEO members, $35 for nonmembers

- *Accounting for Equity Compensation* is a guide to the accounting rules that govern equity compensation programs in the U.S.

  $35 for NCEO members, $50 for nonmembers

- *If I'd Only Known That* is a guide to common mistakes in equity compensation and what to do about them.

  $25 for NCEO members, $35 for nonmembers

- *Equity Compensation for Limited Liability Companies* describes how equity compensation works in an LLC and provides a model plan document.

  $25 for NCEO members, $35 for nonmembers

- *The Stock Options Book* is a straightforward, comprehensive overview covering the legal, accounting, regulatory, and design issues involved in implementing a stock option or stock purchase plan.

  $35 for NCEO members, $50 for nonmembers

- *Selected Issues in Equity Compensation* is more detailed and specialized than *The Stock Options Book,* with chapters on issues such as repricing, securities issues, and evergreen options.

  $35 for NCEO members, $50 for nonmembers

- *Equity Alternatives: Restricted Stock, Performance Awards, Phantom Stock, SARs, and More* is a complete guide, including annotated model plans, to phantom stock, restricted stock, stock appreciation rights, performance awards, and more. A CD with plan documents is included.

    Price: $35 for NCEO members, $50 for nonmembers

Issue Brief Subscription

Our issue briefs are short publications (8.5 x 11 inches in size and typically 20 to 50 pages long) that address specific topics relevant to employee ownership. When bought individually, they cost $15 each for NCEO members and $25 for nonmembers. With our issue brief subscription, you can receive each new issue brief at a low cost: $50 per year for NCEO members and $75 for nonmembers in PDF format, or $75 per year for NCEO members and $100 for nonmembers in hard-copy format (for non-U.S. residents, the hard-copy version is $150 for members and $200 for nonmembers).

To join the NCEO as a member or to order publications, use the order form on the following page, order online at www.nceo.org, or call us at 510-208-1300. If you join at the same time you order publications, you will receive the members-only publication discounts.

Order Form

This book is published by the National Center for Employee Ownership (NCEO). You can order additional copies online at our Web site, www.nceo.org; by telephoning the NCEO at 510-208-1300; by faxing this page to the NCEO at 510-272-9510; or by sending this page to the NCEO at 1736 Franklin Street, 8th Floor, Oakland, CA 94612. If you join as an NCEO member with this order, or are already an NCEO member, you will pay the discounted member price for any publications you order.

Name

Organization

Address

City, State, Zip (Country)

Telephone Fax Email

Method of Payment: ❑Check (payable to "NCEO") ❑Visa ❑M/C ❑AMEX

Credit Card Number

Signature Exp. Date

Checks are accepted only for orders from the U.S. and must be in U.S. currency.

Title	Qty.	Price	Total

Tax: California residents add 8.75% sales tax (on publications only, not membership)

Shipping: In the U.S., first publication $5, each add'l $1; elsewhere, we charge exact shipping costs to your credit card, plus a $10 handling surcharge; no shipping charges for membership

Introductory NCEO Membership: $90 for one year ($100 outside the U.S.)

Subtotal	$
Sales Tax	$
Shipping	$
Membership	$
TOTAL DUE	$